Lucy Herbert

Several methods and practices of devotion, Superior of the English Augustin Nuns

appertaining to a religious life

Lucy Herbert

Several methods and practices of devotion, Superior of the English Augustin Nuns
appertaining to a religious life

ISBN/EAN: 9783742840653

Manufactured in Europe, USA, Canada, Australia, Japa

Cover: Foto ©Lupo / pixelio.de

Manufactured and distributed by brebook publishing software (www.brebook.com)

Lucy Herbert

Several methods and practices of devotion, Superior of the English Augustin Nuns

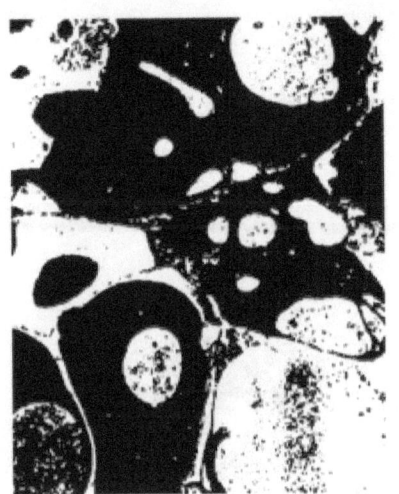

SEVERAL METHODS

AND

PRACTICES

OF

DEVOTION:

APPERTAINING TO A

RELIGIOUS LIFE.

COLLECTED TOGETHER

BY THE

Right Hon. Lady LUCY HERBERT,

Of POWIS,

Superior of the English Augustin Nuns.

PRINTED IN THE YEAR 1791.

Maria Eleanora Giffard / × × × 1807

SEVERAL METHODS
AND
PRACTICES
OF
DEVOTION:
APPERTAINING TO A
RELIGIOUS LIFE.

CHAP. I.
OF PRAYER.
SEC. I.

The great advantages and benefit of it.

PRAYER is the means which God gives us to attain to our last end; and to that sanctity and perfection he has designed us. 'Tis of such profit, that a damned soul would suffer all her torments,

ments, and twice as much, till the day of Judgement, to have the fruit thereof.

Our Holy Father, St. Auguſtin, ſays, 'Tis the key of all God's heavenly treaſures. How much does our poverty and want of all good ſtand in need of ſuch a key!

'Tis the channel by which God's graces are conveyed into our ſouls. 'Tis compared to Jacob's Ladder, by means of which our ſouls aſcend to God; we by it learning to know, love, and adore him; and he deſcends to us by his graces, and the knowledge he gives us of our nothing.

As the body walks on its feet, ſo the ſoul walks towards God by her three powers in Prayer.

By Prayer our ſouls become the Kingdom of God, whoſe Throne raiſed in our hearts, is that of his mercy; and God becomes to us what we pleaſe ourſelves, as we do to him.

Prayer is, to a devout Chriſtian, a bottomleſs treaſure, ſo that he may ſay with truth, that in that one he has all other bleſſings. 'Tis by Prayer that God is moved to execute all thoſe favourable deſigns his mercy has over us.

There is nothing that Prayer can aſk, and Heaven can refuſe; neither relief to the

the poor, nor comfort to the afflicted, nor victory to the oppreſt, nor grace and pardon to ſinners, nor any virtue to the juſt: in a word, whoever knows how to aſk what he wants, can never want what he aſks.

Prayer is the greateſt bleſſing that Heaven can beſtow; 'tis a blank ſigned by Almighty God, wherein we may write what requeſt we pleaſe, with a full ſecurity that it is granted, if we perform our part.

By Prayer only thoſe graces are obtained, neceſſary towards the Salvation of moſt, nay of all, according to our Holy Father; for the grace of perſeverance is neceſſary to Salvation, and it is never given but to thoſe who obtain it by their Prayers: for the Juſt could no more perſevere without God's ſpecial aſſiſtance, than they could acquire virtue without his merciful grace.

Prayer brings a perſon to the perfection God calls her to: there is not a bleſſing of Heaven which flows not through that channel.

SEC. II.

Of the Necessity of Prayer, chiefly mental.

The Prayers Christ made for us, tho' of themselves so forcible; and the Sacrifices of himself offered for us, though of an infinite value; must be applied to us, or they will avail us nothing; and they are only applied to us by our Prayers and Sacrifices offered to him.

St. Gregory says that Prayer is the principal means that the Divine Providence makes use of to execute what God has designed us from all Eternity, but will not give us without being asked.

Unless we become persons of Prayer, we shall never attain perfection nor the love of God.

It is by means of Prayer that we reform what corrupt nature continually produces in our hearts; it is therefore called the murderer of vices and the nursery of virtues. If we find in our souls any passion or evil inclination which troubles her peace, it is in Prayer we must find a remedy, as well as to whatever may hinder our progress in virtue.

As

As we are by our state obliged to tend to perfection, so consequently we are obliged to use mental Prayer, and, according to the progress we make therein, we may judge of that we make in perfection.

Food is not more necessary to maintain our corporal life, than Prayer is to maintain the spiritual life of our souls; which consists in knowing and loving God.

The reason, if there is but few Saints in religious Communities, is because few apply themselves to Prayer as they ought. A person addicted to Prayer, though without learning, and of few or no talents, shall produce wonders in advancing God's glory and drawing souls to him; whereas another with learning, and more talents, shall produce no such fruit.

A servant of God used to say, that by his Morning Prayer he could tell what the rest of the day would be; which shews the necessity of our well performing that duty.

Nothing will be a greater regret to us in purgatory, nay in Heaven, (if we could be capable of grief there) than not to have employed the time of Prayer as we ought; since by it we might have obtained what we stood in need of, and enriched ourselves with all we wanted; God having promised to deny nothing that we should ask praying.

After Christ's Baptism, the Heavens were only opened when he prayed; to teach us that, after baptismal grace, no other is obtained but by Prayer, and consequently how necessary Prayer is.

SEC. III.

Of the Use we must make of Aridities and Distractions in mental Prayer.

We must first understand that the gift of Prayer is a gift of God, which is not acquired by human industry; but his Divine Majesty gives it, and that only to the humble, who persevere to present themselves before him with an intention and desire to do their best to please him, entirely abandoning themselves to his providence.

By the gift of Prayer is meant a facility to raise our thoughts and unite our minds to God; and to make solid reflections, conceive good affections, and express

express ourselves to his Divine Majesty, by interior words and sentiments produced from the heart.

We must make a difference between the success of our Prayer and our application to it. The first depends no more on us, than the rain depends on the earth, but it depends on God alone. The second depends on us with the help of God's grace, we labouring as the sower does, but expecting the increase and growth only from God.

If God draws us to some affection as soon as we are placed in his presence, we must not fix ourselves to the points proposed, but follow that affection as long as we find ourselves drawn by it.

We must not lose courage nor be dejected, when so dry that our understanding cannot discourse of any thing, nor our will find any affection or gust; but in this case we ought, now and then, to lift up our minds to God by short aspirations; as for example:

We endeavour to discourse upon the first point of our meditation, and nothing occurs, let us lift up our minds to God and say, *O my God! your will be done*; then endeavour to discourse again, and if nothing

thing occurs, say, *My God, I wish I could love and serve you better.* Then try again, and if the same, say, *Dear Lord, you know what I am, for you made me: I would fain be able to entertain you, but my weakness and stupidity is so great, that I find myself incapable of being united to you in mind, or keeping my thoughts upon the subject of my meditation.*

This done, endeavour to bring back your thoughts with peace and quiet to the subject of your meditation; forcing yourself to remain with respect and submission in the presence of God, kneeling humbly with your hands joined; and if you still wander from the subject, and are as dry as before, produce again some such aspirations, till your time allotted for prayer is ended.

God is not displeased nor angry with us for the distractions we have against our will; but rather has compassion of us and is pleased, if at the sight of them we humble ourselves, and endeavour to bring back our thoughts to him. And tho' we should be distracted a hundred times, we must not trouble ourselves, but sweetly put ourselves in his presence again, as if nothing had happened; and never make reflections

reflections upon what distracted us, neither by interior lamentations or contrary acts, for that were to imprint them more in our mind.

Although, during the time of Prayer, we did nothing else but withdraw our minds from distractions, and sweetly replace ourselves in the presence of God, fixing our thoughts again on our subject of meditation; yet should we have employed our time not less profitably and meritoriously, than if we had been interiorly recollected the whole time, because we did what was in our power, and God, who requires no more, will not fail sooner or later to recompense our fidelity if we persevere in so doing, and that perhaps with the gift of Prayer.

This gift of Prayer is one of the greatest gifts that God bestows on earth to souls that are faithful to him; and those who know its value, will prefer it to that of Prophecy and working Miracles, and to all other gifts. That soul to whom God gives it, is rich for her life, and more rich than those who have the gift of knowledge, eloquence, and learning, for a person of Prayer is the object of God's complaisance;

complaisance; it is with her he takes his delights.

But whatever degree of perfection we are arrived to, we must not of ourselves presume higher than the common sort of Prayer, which consists in meditation, affection, and good purposes, or resolutions: our study must be to labour couragiously for solid virtue, and especially the mortification of our passions. As to a higher Prayer, God will raise us to it when he sees his time, and so much the sooner, as we seek it less, and remain in the humble knowledge of our nothing and unworthiness: it is then he will probably say to us, *Amice ascende superius.* Friend ascend up higher.

What we must seek in Prayer, is only God, and to pay our duty to him; neither expect nor desire great lights, or such like favours, but only the pure love of God, and of his Cross. Commonly the greatest falls in Holy souls have been after the greatest consolations. Yet we must not contemn sensible devotion under pretence that it brings no solid virtue, for though this be true in effect, yet it helps much to virtue, and Saints have made great profit by consolations.

This

This we must be convinced of, that Prayer without mortification is a meer illusion and fancy. It is by Prayer that we must learn to mortify ourselves, and therefore we must not esteem that time lost which has been spent in aridity and resisting distractions, for then we practise mortification, which is the fruit of Prayer.

The securest mortifications and penances, according to the testimony of several holy and experienced persons, is interior recollection and Prayer; so that few or none, if they consulted nature, would not rather employ the like time in the most painful corporal labour; because that so the natural liberty of thinking is thereby constrained, our appetite suppress, our motions restrained, our will tied up, and our mind attentive not to give entrance to any thing that may distract or trouble the repose of our souls: in short, the whole is under a constraint which is very painful.

SEC. IV.

Of Preparation for Prayer.

Preparation for Prayer is absolutely necessary; without it we tempt God, as the Holy Scripture says, by inconsiderately performing an action of so great importance; which Christ has merited for us with his precious blood and death, in order to attain to that degree of glory designed for us. This ought to raise in us a great confidence of obtaining what we want and pray for; and also a care not to mispend or lose so precious a time.

The Remote Preparation.

This Remote Preparation is first a high esteem of Prayer, often begging the gift of it. 2dly, Mortification, especially of our passions. 3dly, Purity of heart. And lastly, Interior recollection, elevating our thoughts to God from time to time.

Over night we should foresee the points we are next day to meditate upon, and endeavour to imprint them well in our mind; and see what bent and inclination we will endeavour to give to our hearts.

As we go to Prayer we may imagine those words of the Prophet spoke to us: *God expects you to do you mercy.* Let us dispose ourselves for it, in the spirit of Sacrifice, seeking only to content God.

SEC. V.

SEC. V.

What we are to observe in Time of Prayer.

This familiar comparison may instruct us how we ought to comport ourselves before Almighty God in Prayer, even as a blind person would do, if in the presence of the King: He does not see him, but as soon as he is told the King is present, he puts himself, and remains in a respectful posture. If the King does him the honour to call him, he approaches, and the firm belief that it is the King he speaks to, hinders him from thinking of any thing else. He forms in his mind no other idea but that of the King, and is wholly attentive to him. So in like manner ought we to behave ourselves in time of Prayer.

In that time our body must be composed in an humble manner, and our souls must come accompanied with faith, hope, and charity; these will put it in the posture and situation which it ought to be in, in order to speak and converse with God.

Being on our knees, we must adore God present, and offer ourselves entirely to him, together with our Prayer; to his greater glory, and the accomplishment of all his merciful designs over us, and for whatever other intention or person we design to offer it.

Then beg the grace of the Holy Ghost, through the merits of Christ, and of his Sacred spouse the Blessed Virgin, and say, O my dear Jesus, I give you my heart to praise, adore, and love you; and I unite it with your intentions and affections, make me partaker of them, I beseech you.

We must always make two preludes; then Meditation, Affection, Resolutions, and Colloquies, which together compose mental Prayer. The chief acts to be made in time of it are, Faith, Hope, Charity, Adoration, Admiration, Praise, Thanksgiving, Confidence, Contrition, Diffidence in ourselves, Petition, and Resolution.

SEC. VI.

After Prayer.

We must, for the space of a *Miserere* or two, reflect upon our Prayer, to see in what we have been wanting. If we made our two preludes, and with what respect the first, and fervour the second. Whether our memory did its duty by endeavouring to remember the subject we were to meditate upon. And if our understanding were not deficient in discoursing upon the matter; or whether we strayed from it through negligence. If our will was not wanting in raising conformable affections. Lastly, What fruit we drew from our meditation, and when, and how we shall practise it.

Then return thanks to the Divine Majesty, for having permitted you to remain so long in his presence; and for all the graces he has bestowed upon you during that time. Beg pardon for all the faults you have committed, and the grace to practise what he has moved you to resolve on; sensible that of yourself you can do nothing.

Whatever fault you are sensible you have committed, endeavour to amend it in your afternoon's meditation, which, generally speaking, should be a repetition of the morning one.

SEC. VII.

SEC. VII.

Preludes which may serve for any Meditation.

1st Prelude. Imagine yourself at the feet of Jesus crucified.

The 2d Prelude, Is to beg of our crucified Saviour, light to understand the truth proposed, and the grace to form such acts and resolutions as may be most pleasing to him, and conformable to his Divine Will; and may influence not only all the actions of the following day, but also of our whole life.

SEC. VIII.

A Second Manner when before the Blessed Sacrament.

The first Prelude is, To adore, with a firm Faith, Jesus Christ present in the Blessed Sacrament, who, when on earth, taught us by his own example the virtue we are to meditate on; or else with his own mouth taught us the doctrine or truth proposed.

The

The second Prelude is, To thank him for the example he gave us of it; and to beg he will please to give us light to understand it, and grace to practise it the remainder of our life.

SEC. IX.

A Third Manner.

The first Prelude is, To cast a thought upon the whole subject of the Meditation.

The second, To ask of Almighty God, by a fervent aspiration, the virtue we seek by it.

SEC. X.

A Compendium of mental Prayer.

1st, Preparation has three parts, presence of God, choice of matter, and invocation.

2dly, Meditation has three parts, Consideration, Affection, and Resolution.

3dly, Conclusion has three parts, Thanksgiving, Oblation, and Petition.

SEC. XI.

SEC. XI.

Different Manners of Meditating.

The first may be to reduce our Meditations to these three points. The first point proposes the truth or precept. The second point is to reflect on what is to be done to reduce this precept to practice. And the third point is Petition, by way of colloquy.

In the first point we must endeavour to imprint in our heart and mind the truth proposed, weighing the motives, conceiving the importance, making upon it acts of faith, &c.

In the second point we must reflect upon the different practices, and chuse that which may best suit with our state and condition; foreseeing the different occasions we shall have of practising it, and resolving upon it, taking our measures accordingly.

The third point is, Prayer or Petition, which must come from the heart, and this not only during the time of meditation, but from time to time the rest of the day, which will serve not only to keep

keep us in the presence of God, but also will mind us of the resolutions we made in Prayer.

SEC. XII.

A Second Manner of Prayer.

Is to reduce our Meditation to these four following points.

The 1st Point must be all the motives than can raise an esteem or desire of the virtue we meditate on.

The second point is to reflect what one in our circumstances would do, that was resolved to obtain and practise that virtue.

The third point is to reflect whether we do so or no, and take a view of the faults we commit against it, with contrition for them.

The fourth point is to consider what we will do hereafter; together with all the purposes relating to that virtue; and earnestly beseech Almighty God to grant us the grace of it.

SEC. XIII.

SEC. XIII.

A Third Manner of Prayer, consisting in six Points.

1st Point, Is a simple view of the truth we are to meditate on, putting it before the eye of our mind, and by an act of faith believing it to be such as it is revealed to us.

2d Point, Is Consideration upon the same matter.

3d Point, Consists in Affections of the will.

4th Point, In Reflections on ourselves.

5th Point, In Resolutions.

And the 6th Point, In Petitions.

SEC. XIV.

A fourth Manner of Prayer when we meditate on a Command, Precept, or any Obligation.

1st Point, Is to consider the nature of it, and in what it obliges.

2d Point, How we have observed it, and in what we have violated it.

3d Point,

3d Point, Is to be sorry for the faults we have committed, and conclude with colloquies, heartily begging it of Almighty God, and beseeching our Lady to obtain it for us.

SEC. XV.

A fifth Manner, when we make our Meditation upon some Virtue.

1st Point, Is to give thanks for the example Christ has given us of that virtue in himself and in his Saints.

2d Point, Is to beg light to know the necessity, excellency, and advantages of it, and how we should practise it; taking a view of our faults against it.

3d Point, Is to purpose amendment, marking the time, place, and occasion of practising it, concluding with one or two colloquies.

The same is to be observed in meditating upon any sentence or maxim, for either it contains some virtue to be embraced, or some vice to be avoided.

If a virtue, 1st. its Nature; 2d. its Qualities; 3d. the Example of those who have excelled in it; and 4th. the contrary vice.

If a Vice, 1st. its Nature; 2d. its Causes; 3d. its Effects; 4th. the Wrong it does to God.

SEC. XVI.

A sixth Manner, considering the Faculties of our soul, or senses of our body.

1st Point, To reflect on the use of those Faculties.

2d Point, To see if we make that use of them.

3d Point, To ask pardon and purpose amendment, concluding with colloquies.

SEC. XVII.

A very profitable way of meditating by consideration of a Crucifix.

First imagine yourself at the foot of our Saviour's Cross, and having adored him, and prostrated yourself in mind before him, lift up your eyes and consider his five wounds.

At the right hand repass in your mind all the benefits you have received from his infinite bounty; they are the purchase of the Blood that runs from the Sacred Wound; thank the Divine Author.

At the left hand, consider the adversities and afflictions, which by his providence have happened to you; express your grief for not having received them, as coming from his sacred hand, with due patience and resignation. Beg grace to do better for the future.

At the right foot, consider the good works you have done by means of the grace purchased for you by the merits of that Sacred Wound; see if they are full, done with a pure intention, and consider what good you might have done, and have not, because you would not.

At the left foot, consider how injurious you have been to that Sacred Wound, in the many sins you have committed against God, your neighbour, and yourself, all which has pierced that foot you behold, and caused him more pain than the nail. Beg pardon and grace to amend.

At the Sacred Wound of the side, see what your desires and love are; then at least open your heart, and fetch out of it affections of sorrow, love, and gratitude.

SEC. XVIII.

Another Manner.

After having prostrated yourself at the feet of Jesus, and paid him your respects, lift up your eyes, and consider all the parts of his Sacred Body one after another.

Then think of the pain and dolour he suffered in that part; as for example, in his hands, and that for the love of you. That thought will produce affections of sorrow, compassion, thanks, love, &c.

Then cast your eyes on your own hands, and consider the sins you have committed with them. Grieve, beg pardon, and purpose amendment.

Foresee the acts of virtue which you may perform with your hands for the love of Jesus, and purpose to do so in the first occasion. Beg the God of bounty to favour you with his grace.

After this manner you may pass over all the parts of his Sacred Body, making the same reflections, and reciting a *Pater* and *Ave* after each.

SEC. XIX.

A Manner.

Which is by a simple view of the Mysteries of our Saviour's Life. As this is most easy, so it is most devout. You need only run over our Lord's life, stopping at the principal parts, and making acts of Faith, Adoration, Love, Contrition, Thanks, Offering, Petition, and Hope.

You must always observe the three following things: 1st, Not to look on the Mystery you meditate upon as past, but present, since it is so in the idea of God; and though the action is past, the virtue of it is not, nor the love with which Christ wrought it; for his love is infinite, immutable, and ever the same; and as ardent now, as when he gave his Life and Blood, being still ready to do the same if it were necessary.

2dly, If you find in any one mystery wherewithal to entertain yourself devoutly, go no further, but remain therein as long as your devotion lasts.

3dly, After each Mystery say a *Pater* and *Ave*.

In all Meditations the memory muſt remember the matter, and repreſent the points to the underſtanding according to the manner we have prepared them, making an Act of Faith touching the truth contained in them; then the underſtanding conſiders the perſons, the nature, the place, the time, the end, the means, and the manner. And the will produces proper acts and affections.

SEC. XX.

To perform an Act of Thankſgiving well.

We muſt conſider the perſon that beſtows the gift, who is a God of an infinite dignity. 2dly, On whom he beſtows it, to wit, on a poor miſerable creature. 3dly, The value of the gift. 4thly, The love with which it is given. 5thly, The diſintereſtedneſs of the giver.

Then we muſt unite our thankſgiving with that which Chriſt in this world rendered to his eternal Father, for all favours beſtowed on him, and on us all; and which he daily continues to render him in the moſt Bleſſed Sacrament.

SEC. XXI.

The Manner of making Colloquies in Prayer.

A Colloquy is nothing else but a serious treaty with Almighty God, our Blessed Lady, any Saint, or our Angel Guardian, wherein the soul uses all the arguments she can to move and incline God, or his Saints, to be propitious to her; to which she is excited by her extreme need, and invited to have recourse to his Divine Majesty by these kind invitations. *Come to me all you that labour, &c. Knock, and it shall be opened, &c. Come and buy of me burning gold; come and you shall have it gratis. My delights are to be with the children of men. When I shall be exalted, I will draw all to myself.* All which evidently shews that God is desirous to give audience to a soul, if she humbly sues for it. 1st, In pleading, our first argument may be drawn from God himself, or from his power.

You can, O my God, do whatsoever you will. Were I able to effect that which you can by your will alone, I would instantly make myself wholly yours,

yours, and remain so for ever: shall I say this with truth, and yet be refused and rejected by you, when I know that you desire it more than I do? My God, I beseech you, break through those impediments which part us; and once for all make room for your mercies, and possess my soul now at least as you do the souls of your Elect.

2. A second way to move God to shew mercy to us, may be to expose to him our miseries, moving him to it after this manner.

If your mercy, my God, requires misery to cure, that you may shew the bowels of your compassion, who, alas! more miserable than I, that am misery itself, both in soul and body. Behold, therefore, in me an ample subject for your mercy to work on, for misery is the proper object of mercy.

3. A third means to move his Divine Majesty may be drawn from the natural inclination he has to do good to all. Beseech him to follow that inclination in your regard, since he is so much inclined to it; and his treasures, neither of light nor heat, will be diminished by his
vouch-

vouchsafing to enkindle that black coal yourself with the same.

4. A fourth means may be taken from the merits of Christ in this manner.

I do not deny, my God, that I have offended you, and that I deserve nothing but darkness and destruction. But is it possible that my sins, how many or great soever they be, can anyways counterpoise the merits of my Saviour? Be pleased, therefore, to lay my sins, for which I deserve your wrath, in the balance against his merits, and you will see how much they out-weigh my crimes. Did I believe my sins greater than your Goodness and Mercy, as Cain did, there might be reason to confound me; but I declare on the contrary that your Mercy is incomparably greater: Therefore I beg you to receive the merits of your Son, and discharge me of all my Debts and Sins; where else can I possibly go, and who can help me but you?

5. A fifth manner of pleading may be to shew the title we have to all the treasures and merits of Christ's Life and Death, they being ours by his free gift. Let us reckon upon each of his Thoughts, Words, Deeds, Affections, Intentions, and

and Motions, for the space of thirty-three years: those infinite treasures he stored up for us. We may urge how little of any of them will serve our turn, seeing that one only thought of his, or tear, or word, is of an infinite value, and sufficient for millions of souls. And to apply any of them to our necessities, there needs no more but one word, or *Fiat,* how easy then for him to do it!

6. We may make use of the merits of the Blessed Mother of God, producing all her titles of honour; those in her Litanies are nearest at hand, and full of solid arguments, either to incline herself, or her dearest Son, to grant or favour our request. Nothing will move more than the affections of her heart, especially those she had when she accompanied her Divine Son in his Sacred Passion, and stood by his cross. With them we may buy of God what we stand in need of. It very much imports us to get her to plead our cause, for she never intercedes in vain; because she can move her Son to apply his and the Saints merits to us, and thus enrich us if she pleases.

7. Another manner to move God to help us, may be to alledge what we are of ourselves,

ourselves, how unable to do any thing without the Divine assistance. Let us sink into the very bottom of our own nothing, and set before the eyes of our Lord, or his Mother, or his Saints, (according to the colloquy we make) the whole state of our soul, telling them how things go with us, and leading them through the powers of our soul, as thro' an hospital, letting them see how impossible it is for us to recover or subsist without their help, and what a fair occasion they have to shew their charity, their power, and their skill, perhaps not the like again in the whole world.

Here is to be noted, that in treating thus with our Lord, with his Mother, or with his Saints, many things may occur by way of objection, which may perhaps daunt or discourage a poor soul, if they be not well answered. As the memory of her many sins, her great ingratitude, her fair promises without effect, her extreme tepidity, and sloth in setting hand to work, some habitual imperfections of long continuance, which she seeks not to amend, or gives over as desperate; her diffidence in God's goodness, her want of a lively faith, a certain imagination
that

that God hears her not, a hard conceit of God, &c.

If God objects these things, and complains that you have tied his hands, your answer must be, that he knows that none has the power to do it unless he himself will. And that you will not allow, till such time as it shall appear, that you can be more wicked than he is good, which is impossible.

It much imports us to conceive his infinite goodness bent and inclined to do good by its own nature. This confidence in God is of great advantage to a soul; for when once this virtue enlarges, and extends itself so far as to be, as it were, sure that God will not fail to give her that which she asks, this is ever a kind of obtaining the very thing desired.

We must be convinced that Almighty God, by his own nature, is infinitely liberal; and is delighted to have his children constrain him, as it were, by their importunities, to grant that which he so much desires to give. He would have us esteem ourselves his children, nay his darling children, to whom he will refuse nothing that may be for their good.

To

To conclude, these things here set down may serve a soul very much in Prayer. They are insinuated to open a way as it were, and shew in what manner it may be effected. They are also of a most excellent use in time of darkness and desolation, and will bring much succour and relief for the enabling poor creatures to go through such dryness and discomforts as sometimes it pleases Almighty God to permit a soul to feel.

SEC. XXII.

Some methods which may serve in desolation and dryness, to prevent losing one's time.

1st. Is that which Saint Theresia used in the beginning of her application to Prayer, being easy and profitable. It is to read a little in a spiritual book; then pause a while to imprint it in your mind, and endeavour to draw some good affections and resolutions from it.

2d. Is almost like the first, and is recommended by St. Ignatius. Take some sentence of Scripture, or any vocal Prayer. As the *Pater, Ave, Credo,* and say it leisurely, either vocally or in your heart; stay

stay upon each word as long as you find the affections or sentiments of piety, which it raises in your mind, entertain you. At the end beg some grace or virtue conformable to what you have meditated.

3. A third way is, when the subject prepared, furnishes not entertainment enough, to fall into some acts, as faith, adoration, thanksgiving, hope, love, &c. which may be made in short and pathethic words, staying upon each as long as it gives any entertainment.

4. A fourth, which is of use when you cannot meditate, or raise any affections on the prepared points. In this sterility you may protest to Almighty God, that you desire to make as many acts of virtue as you shall fetch your breath. Offer his Divine Majesty, in lieu of what you are not able to do, that honour which is rendered him by the Saints in Heaven, and by all his Servants upon earth, especially what they render him at that present time.

5. A fifth is an application of mind, to Jesus in the Blessed Sacrament, which may be done thus: first adore our Saviour
in

in this Divine Myſtery, with all the reſpect his preſence requires.

2dly, Unite yourſelf to him, and to all his Divine operations in the euchariſt, where he inceſſantly adores, loves, and praiſes his Eternal Father in the name of all men, in quality of a victim that is continually ſacrificed. Reflect on his recollection, ſolitude, hidden life, obedience, humility, patience, reſolve, and beg grace to imitate him in occaſions. 3dly, Offer this worthy victim to the Eternal Father, thereby to render him the ſovereign homage you owe him, and to return him worthy thanks for all benefits received, and to ſatisfy his juſtice, and oblige his mercies. 4thly, Conclude by ſpiritual Communion.

This practice is an excellent manner of Prayer, which we ought to make familiar to us, ſince our happineſs in this life conſiſts in, and depends on, our union with Jeſus Chriſt in the Bleſſed Sacrament.

CHAPTER II.

SEC. I.

Motives to raise in us a high esteem of the Divine Office.

THE Divine Office is a manner of Prayer peculiar to Priests and Religious Persons. It is ordained by the Holy Ghost, who governs the Church, for the employment of God's chosen people; that whilst the rest of men are employed in the various distractions of this life, they might be employed in praising, loving, thanking, and petitioning Almighty God, both for themselves and for others.

Another design of our Holy Mother the Church in it, is to imitate the triumphant Church which has, for its continual occupation, to praise God in loving him, and to love him in praising him.

We ought then to perform it with all the reverence a creature can pay to her God; and with all the love a created heart can yield, that being the employment

ment of Angels, and if we are not unhappy, will be ours for Eternity.

What a misery would it be if we should so perform what is ordained to gain our happiness withal, as to merit punishment; and in place of pleasing God, should offend him! for it is either a source of graces, or of misfortune, according as we perform it well or ill. What reward can we expect when the petitions we present are so delivered as to provoke God in place of pleasing him.

Saint Basil tells us the Divine assistance is not to be implored coldly, or with a wandering mind, for those that do so not only miss of the grant of their petitions, but incur his displeasure.

Saint Gregory assures us that God hears not the Prayers to which he who prays attends not: And the reason why so many Priests and Religious Persons remain still burdened with their defects, and make so little progress in perfection, often declining from bad to worse, is their performing this divine duty so negligently; for did they perform it as they ought, they would increase in grace, and thereby in all virtues and perfection.

To perform as we ought, we must do it for God, in God, and with God. It is not sufficient to be present in person, but the heart and soul with all our powers, must be applied to it; for not to perform it so, is to be rather *cryers* than *Prayers*.

We ought to look on the Divine Office as our greatest daily duty and employment, imposed on us by Supreme Power, and accepted of by us; so the performing it well, should be our principal care.

The name it bears shews the excellence of it. It is first called *Divine*, because it was inspired by the Spirit of God, and instituted to praise and worship him. And secondly, it is called *Office*, because it is the charge and office of Ecclesiastical and Religious Persons, whom our Holy Mother the Church deputes as Embassadors from her to Almighty God; to praise, love, and thank him; to beg his pardon, help, and assistance; supply and atone for several of her children who neither love, serve, nor praise him; and also to imitate the triumphant Church.

We may look upon ourselves not only as deputed by the Church, but also by our house and order, to praise God in the

the name of them all; to beg pardon for their sins and offences, and the continuation of his mercies, and of the graces that are necessary for each. Be persuaded that part of the benedictions that God grants the order, are tied to the public Prayers performed in it. Our founders' design in obliging us to the Divine Office was, that those Prayers should have the force to draw God's Blessings on it; have we not then reason to reproach ourselves that our negligent performing it is the cause, if God deprives the community of many graces and benedictions which he would otherways bestow?

The Divine Office may be considered as a tribute which our tongue and heart pays to God; and that which ought to raise our esteem of it is, that it is believed that Christ, when on earth, recited the Psalter according to the custom of the Jews: and when he was on the cross he began the 12th Psalm, *Deus, Deus meus ut quid dereliquisti me*, according to opinion he entirely ended.

We cannot do better than to unite ourselves to our Saviour, while we say or sing the Divine Office, begging him to present our Prayers and Praises with his own to his Eternal Father for his glory and the good of the Church; and at the same time let us beg him, by his all adorable heart, to supply for all the faults we have committed and do commit therein. This he revealed to St. Mechtilda, and St. Gertrude was very pleasing to him.

SEC. II.

Of the Remote Preparation for the Divine Office.

We perform the Divine Office ill, because we do not prevent it by such foreseen considerations as might take up our thoughts, and stir us up to fervour and holy affections.

Though we cannot help being distracted, yet we may be faulty in the cause of the distractions, by omitting to dispose ourselves for Prayer. Yet no other preparation is required, but only as we go to the quire from the first stroke of the bell, to recollect and excite in ourselves a reverential esteem of the duty we are called to perform, which is to speak to God, and that in the most sacred place upon earth,

earth, where God is present to give audience, and favour those that pronounce his praises.

We may reflect as we go, what care a person that was to have audience of the King would take to prepare what he was to say. We are happily void of that trouble, for our Holy Mother the Church puts into our mouths the words we are to speak, which are no other than the King's own words, to whom we are to speak. It was his Holy Spirit that inspired them; all he requires of us is, that our hearts join with the words, otherways his Divine Majesty will have but little regard to the words we speak, (though his own) unless he hears the cries of our hearts, by the desire of pleasing and honouring him.

To excite us to fervour for each part of the Office, we may, as we go to it, make use of these reflections. Going to *Mattins*, reflect with what fervour the same has been performed by several in the night; and if we are excused from performing it then, it is that we may do it with more fervour and alacrity, having had sufficient sleep; and as the design of rising in the night to say it was, tha whilst worldlings took their rest,

Servants and Spouses should be employed in praising him, and atone for the sins and offences committed against him during the night, so that thought should stir us up to a fervorous performance of the same.

In going to *Prime*, let us raise in ourselves a great desire to perform it well, it being the first hour of the Day's Office, and may mind us of the first beginning of our life, from the time we had the use of reason, which ought to have been employed in serving God; and for not having done it, we must redouble our fervour, and enter into the sentiments of the Church, who, by the Prayers of Prime, begs for all her children, that God would not only preserve them from sins, but conduct them, and teach them to observe all his commandments, and sanctify their thoughts, words, and actions.

Tierce is particularly designed to render thanks to God for the sanctification of the Church by means of the Holy Ghost, who descended visibly upon the Apostles at that hour; and also to beg him to continue to animate it with his and his Spirit.

When

When called to the two last hours, excite yourself to sentiments of gratitude, considering God's goodness to you in calling you from time to time to praise him: endeavour to do it with all imaginable fervour.

In going to Vespers reflect on the hour when Christ gave the greatest proof he could give of his love for us, by yielding up his life for our redemption, endeavour for to prove yours by a particular fervour in reciting this part of the Divine Office.

Complin being the conclusion of the Day's Office, ought to be performed with a double diligence, that it may atone for the faults we committed in the rest of our Office; as also to prepare our hearts, by true devotion, to end the day piously.

Our intention must be pure, we must be carried to this Divine Service only by the motive of God's glory, and not for the sensible satisfaction which proceeds from so holy an action.

SEC.

SEC. III.

The immediate Preparation for the Divine Office.

As soon as we enter the quire we must, with profound respect, adore God really present in the most Blessed Sacrament, uniting our adorations with those the Angels render him. Let us also offer him his own thoughts and divine operations, begging he will apply them to us, as he sees most for his own Honour and our Sanctification.

Having made your intention before you begin, beg the grace of Prayer of Almighty God, and invoking the Divine Spirit to pray in you, say, open my lips O my God, that I may bless your Holy name, and purify my heart from all that tends not to your service: enlighten my understanding, and inflame my will, that I may recite this office worthily, devoutly, and attentively, to the end I may deserve to be graciously heard by your Divine Majesty. I offer it united with the Prayers my Saviour offered you when in this world, and with those he now renders

ders you in the adorable Sacrament; and also with all those that are rendered you by the Saints and Angels in Heaven, and by the Faithful upon earth; begging that the perfection of theirs may supply for the defects of mine.

In all vocal Prayers there are three sorts of attention which we may have: the first may be called material, the second spiritual, and the third Divine. The 1st is the least, which is to have attention to pronounce the words well, without missing through want of attention, or confounding one with another through precipitation, which suffices to fulfil the obligation of them that are obliged to the Divine Office, though it renders but little glory to God, and brings small profit to our souls. The 2d is to attend to the sense of the words, and this is more perfect and agreeable to God, and more profitable to ourselves, because it excites holy affections. The 3d and most perfect keeps the soul applied to God, to whom she speaks, either by considering some of his Divine Perfections, or some Mystery of our Saviour's Passion, so that the understanding admits of no other thought, nor the will of any

any other affection, than to please, glorify, love, and thank God.

SEC. IV.

Several Manners of keeping our thought attentive to God during the Divine Office.

We may consider the Divine Office, 1st, As a Sacrifice of praise and homage to God. 2dly, As a Sacrifice of thanksgiving. 3dly, As a Sacrifice of impetration. And 4thly, As a Sacrifice of propitiation. One day in one manner, and another day in another, as it shall stand with our present disposition, and offering it up accordingly.

When we consider it as a Sacrifice of praise and homage to God, we must reflect upon his infinite greatness. He is the Fountain of Sanctity, and requires to be continually praised and honoured by all his creatures with all imaginable Sanctity. It is him we praise in this Divine Duty, and we thereby say to him all he would have us say. May we also say it as he would have us, that is what we must endeavour.

Secondly,

Secondly, We must reflect on the honour he does us, in not only permitting, but even calling us to praise him, which we ought to perform with all respect and fervour.

Those two reflections should make us perform the Divine Office with such an aweful reverence as becomes a creature when she speaks to her God and Creator.

At every *Gloria Patri*, we must redouble our attention, and with all respect adore that Divine *Being*. One in Essence and three in Persons, from which all creatures receive theirs. We may also in reciting it reflect what those words import, to wit, that God may enjoy the same glory he had from all eternity, and will eternally have, which teaches us how great and independent of any creature God's glory is, and that the greatest honour we can render him cannot go beyond wishing that it may be as it was from all Eternity.

When we consider the Office as a Sacrifice of Thanksgiving, we must first offer it for that intention, and during the time of it call to mind all the effects of God's Mercies and Liberalities to ourselves, and to the community we live in:

and so make of those praises a Sacrifice of Thanksgiving for the same. And this because it is an essential duty to thank God for his favours, and we have not otherways time to employ ourselves therein as we ought.

When we consider it as a Sacrifice of Impetration, we must offer it as such, making choice of one thing, or many which we find the greatest want of, and are most moved to seek and find redress for. Our hearts, during the time, must, in the humblest and simplest manner, represent the same to God, whilst, with our mouths, we pronounce the Divine Office, which is appointed by the Church to beg of Almighty God, all that is necessary for her and for her children.

When we consider it as a Sacrifice of Propitiation, after having offered it as such, we must, during the time of it, raise in ourselves a lively apprehension of the greatness and multitude of our offences, which, according to the Psalmist, are more in number than the hairs of our head. Secondly, We must reflect on the Mercies of God, by which he pardons more willingly than he punishes; taking a pleasure to pardon such as with

sorrow

sorrow for having offended him, have recourse to him: let us conceive a hearty sorrow for all our offences against him.

Sometimes we may entertain our thoughts, during the Divine Office, with these three reflections, or with one of them, according as we find ourselves moved. 1st, God's Charity, by which he loves himself with an infinite love; and then his creatures, communicating himself to them a thousand ways. 2dly, God's Justice, which causes him not to leave the least fault unpunished, nor the least virtue unrewarded. 3dly, His admirable and hidden Providence by which he governs all things, and conducts them to their end; extending itself even to a leaf, and to a hair of the head, being present to all.

At another time we may entertain our thoughts with Christ present in the Blessed Sacrament. It is his proper Throne upon earth, where he seats his Holy Humanity to receive our homages. The honour we here render him ought to answer the opprobies and ignomies he received for us on the cross.

We cannot do better, during the Divine Office, than to keep ourselves united to him, joining our thoughts and affections to his, begging him to present them to his Eternal Father, saying rather with heart than mouth, at the end of each Pſalm or hour, I beſeech you, dear Lord, to unite my unworthy Prayers with yours, and to preſent them ſo united to the glory of your Eternal Father.

At other times, according to the Feaſt we ſolemnize; we may entertain our thoughts in reflecting on God's Love, expreſt to us in that Myſtery, moving ourſelves to ſentiments of love and gratitude for the ſame, and offering ourſelves to his Divine Majeſty in return, or whatever we think he may require of us; and begging that the merits of that myſtery may be applied to us.

We may alſo ſometimes entertain ourſelves during the Office with the matter contained in the ſeven Petitions of the *Pater Noſter*, we may uſe one of them for ſo long as we find guſt and ſatisfaction therein; or may change weekly, daily, or at every hour of the Office as they ſtand in order, for the number will correſpond either to the days of the week or hours of the Office.

The

The same method we may observe if we take for subject of our thoughts the seven words our Saviour spoke on the cross; which would be a fit entertainment for Fridays.

As many reflections may rather charge the imagination than help attention, it is more advisable to let our soul sweetly move towards God, making use of any one reflection which may keep us attentive to him, for as long as we find it does so. It were even to be wished that the whole Divine Office were but one Act of Love.

Notwithstanding it is advisable, and even necessary, to make choice of some one reflection or more, which may restrain and fix our vagabond imagination, it will cost us some pains to accustom ourselves to it; but it is a pain well bestowed and full of merit, being taken to glorify God with more reverence and attention.

On Feasts of our Blessed Lady, we may entertain our thoughts during the Office with some of those elogiums in her Litanies, or else with the words of the Angelical Salutation, Chap. v. Sec. 2, using one of those reflections during the whole

whole Office, or changing at each hour, as suits best with our present devotion and disposition.

When we have ended the Divine Office, we should always reflect a little how we have performed it; and beg pardon for the faults and negligences we have been guilty of, and grace to perform it better the next time. In satisfaction for our faults we should say the Prayer ordained by Pope Leo X. or else that which follows:

O Good Jesus, be propitious to me a sinner. I recommend to your heart, full of sweetness and charity, the Office I have now recited with so much tepidity, and so many distractions. Be pleased to pardon the faults I have therein committed, and to supply for my defect accept of your own merits, which I offer you, and in which I put my total trust and confidence.

In order to satisfy ourselves, we must understand, that although our minds should be so taken up with any of the foregoing reflections, or any such like pious thoughts, for many Psalms together, so as not to reflect on the Psalm, yet provided we say it, we should fulfil our

our obligation, and that with more perfection than if we only attended to them.

A servant of God used, at the end of every *Gloria Patri*, to add these words, *Pater Cœlestis da mihi Spiritum bonum.* Celestial Father, give me your Holy Spirit.

CHAP. III.

SEC. I.

Motives to incline us to frequent visits of the most Blessed Sacrament.

ST. Theresia appearing to one after her death said, that Christ should be to us in the Blessed Sacrament what the Divine Essence is to the Blessed in Heaven, whose whole occupation is to contemplate, adore, and love, so should we comport ourselves to Jesus on our Altars.

Love and gratitude to Christ, whose love for us makes him remain constantly in our Tabernacle, should draw us continually to him. We may look on the Altar as the place where he every day is born, dies, and is offered in Sacrifice for us, applying unto us the fruits of the Blood he has shed for us.

Our

Our frequent visiting him in this his Throne of love is highly pleasing to him, because we comply with his desire, not an ordinary desire, but a vehement, ardent, passionate one, which he expresses by his remaining continually with us, and declaring that his delights are to be with the children of men. Ought not we then to delight in frequently visiting him who, for our sakes, descends from Heaven to earth, and that so frequently? What great matter is it for us to go from our cells, or from any part of the house to visit him, when not hindered by any regular duty?

The Queen of Saba thought it worth her pains to come even from the extremities of the earth, to hear the wisdom of Solomon; and shall we think much of going a few steps to visit Christ our Saviour, who remains in our Tabernacle for our sakes? If we are assiduous in visiting him, we shall undoubtedly receive from him what that Queen received from Solomon, of whom it is said that *He gave her all that she asked, or would.* Reflect a little on those words *asked, or would,* and consider what an advantage you may make by visiting him.

What

What could move Christ, after he had perfectly accomplished the work of our Redemption, to remain still upon earth? nothing but his love and tenderness for us, whom he knew to stand in need of him, as being sick, weak, afflicted, fearful of his judgements; and therefore he would stay with us that we might find in him a Father to comfort us, a Physician to cure us, a Master to teach us, and clear our doubts; a Redeemer to save us; are we not then infinitely blameable if we make not this use of him?

Before the coming of Christ, would any one have thought it possible that a God so great and dreadful, who was then called the God of vengeance, should, out of his pure love to us, not only become man like us, but also make himself our food and nourishment? if this be astonishing, as indeed it is, it is not less wonderful that we should be so insensible and ungrateful as to go seldom near him, when we might do it with so much facility.

Had it been in our choice to have asked some favour, or mark of Christ's love and goodness for us, could we have presumed to have asked such a favour as his

his remaining for ever with us? but what we should not have dared to ask, he has had the goodness to do, knowing how necessary his presence was for us; which makes our ungratefulness in visiting him seldom appear the more.

What excuse can there be for religious persons, lodged under the same roof with Christ, if they do not frequently visit him, they having so many fair opportunities of doing it, and neglecting the same, is the reason why they do but creep, as it were, in the way of perfection; because that is, of all others, the most powerful means to bring them to it, and that means they neglect. A religious man confess'd that nothing more sensibly afflicted him at his death than this.

As there is nothing more beneficial to us than frequently to visit the Blessed Sacrament, so there is no Devotion more pleasing to Almighty God, than our coming to visit and adore him in that his throne of love, which if we are careful to do, we may be assured we shall, thro' the merits of Christ, continue the same for all eternity.

There are an infinity of motives which oblige us frequently to visit Christ in the most

most Blessed Sacrament, yet they may be contained in these few words, *We can do nothing without him; and with him we can do all things.*

SEC. II.

On visiting the most Blessed Sacrament.

It will be better and more profitable to our souls to make fewer visits to the Blessed Sacrament, (as three a day) and spend in each half a quarter of an hour, than to pretend to make more, and make them in a hurry. The properest time for them will be one in the morning, another in the afternoon, and the third before night. And, as much as may be, we should be constant to the time, unless for some just cause we are obliged to advance or defer our visits.

It is the pious practice of many, before they begin their prayers, to address themselves to their good Angel, begging him to join with them, and help them to pray well, which we may do in these or the like words:

O blessed Angel, my faithful Guardian, you know much better than I, what respect

spect and reverence is due to my Divine Saviour in this Sacrament of love; you also know my obligations to him. I beg you to act the part of the best of friends to me, by requesting for me all I stand in need of, helping me to petition the same, and supplying for all my defects. Obtain my Saviour's blessing on my poor endeavours, that they may succeed to his honour and glory, and the good of my soul.

SEC. III.

Manner of visiting the most Blessed Sacrament for every day of the week.

On Sunday the first visit.

Consider Christ in the Blessed Sacrament as your Saviour. Reflect how many ways he has been a Saviour to you. Nothing is more powerful to gain our hearts than this amiable name, and the firm persuasion that he will be a Saviour to us. Therefore the enemy labours to make us doubt of it, thereby to diminish his love in us.

Our Holy Mother the Church assures us that he died for the Salvation of all. With

With what love will this assurance inflame your heart! make an Act of Faith upon this truth, and say,

O my God, I firmly believe that you truly desire my salvation, and died for it. Nothing shall ever make me doubt thereof. Since then you so much desire it, I confide you will grant me all that is necessary for it, and above all your love. For the hell you threaten me with, if I don't love you, has nothing in it so dreadful as that want of your love. Nor the Heaven you have prepared for me, if I do love you, has nothing in it so delightful as that love. Grant me but your love, and I desire no more. And since the accomplishing of your will, and observing your precepts, is the rule you give me of shewing my love, I beg your grace that I may be exact in every point of the same, that there I may truly prove I love you. Increase your love daily in me, I beseech you; and if I am not worthy to die of it, at least I beg I may be so happy as to die in it, and that my last breath may be an act of love to you.

After which, make these following Acts of Faith, Hope, and Charity.

My God, I firmly believe all that faith teaches me concerning your being an infinite good and infinite in all perfections, and I believe that I owe you all my love, all I am, and all I am capable of.

I hope and expect from your infinite goodness and mercy, the remission of all my sins, and all the graces I stand in need of to remain for ever faithful to your love, and to overcome all your enemies and mine.

An Act of charity after these two will be easily made: No matter in how few words exprest, provided it comes from the heart.

Then communicate Spiritually.

Though it be less efficacious than to do it Sacramentally, yet the good it procures us is so considerable, that we cannot omit it without doing a great prejudice to our own souls, for by it God bestows great graces on them.

If

If interest did not engage us as often as we visit the Blessed Sacrament, to receive Christ spiritually, love ought to do it: Since he remains there for our sakes, and expresses the desire he has that we receive him. To comply with it, we must dispose ourselves by an act of humility, and of contrition for our heart by an inflamed desire to receive him, that he may enter and we be united to him.

After which say the following Prayer, which St. Gertrude daily recited in honour of the Heart of Jesus.

I adore you, O Sacred Heart of Jesus, Source of Eternal Life, Treasure of the Divinity, Furnace of Love. You are my only Refuge! O amiable Saviour, inflame my Heart with that love which yours is inflamed with. Pour into my Heart those graces, of which yours is the Source; and grant that my Heart may be so united with yours, that your will may be mine, and that mine may be eternally conformed to yours; which from henceforward I beg may be the rule of all my desires and actions.

*The second Visit for the same Day.
In the Spirit of Confidence.*

Go to your Saviour with sentiments of an entire confidence; as to the certain remedy of all your evils, and source of all your good; for whatever situation or state your soul is in, you will draw great advantage if you thus visit him. Our Holy Father says there is no mortal sin, however horrible, which the death of Jesus cannot blot out. I cannot, says the same Saint, be frightened at the multitude of my Sins, if I call to mind the death of Christ, for that can do more for me than my sins can do against me. In all my adversities, says he, I never found a more efficacious remedy than to have recourse to the wounds of my Saviour, in them I repose without fear.

We cannot entertain ourselves better, nor please our Saviour more, than by exciting in ourselves a perfect confidence in him, asking it of him, and a heart conformable to his, that may always trust and confide in him.

Having excited yourself to this confidence, make the acts of Faith, Hope, and Charity,

Charity, then Spiritual Communion. And St. Gertrude's Prayer as in the first Visit.

The third Visit for the same Day, which may likewise serve for the third Visit of every Day.

It is to confer with our Saviour about all our affairs.

Go to Jesus in the most Blessed Sacrament, to open your heart to him, and to tell him all your concerns, as to your Father and best of friends. Speak to him of your spiritual concerns, and likewise of your temporal ones, for he is not tired with hearing our complaints and miseries.

Speak to him of what passes in your interior. Of the sins and faults you commit, notwithstanding your purposes to the contrary. Of the violent propensions of your corrupt nature, which causes many evils. Of the passions and inclinations which trouble you, &c. And you will doubtless experience the same goodness which they did, who addressed themselves to Christ for their bodily maladies when he was upon earth. Say to him

him with the leper, *Lord, if you will you can cure me.*

If any one has offended you, tell him of it, and learn of him how to comport yourself towards the person. If any particular thing is to be done, consult with him about it; beg his assistance and blessing on it. And when ended, if it succeed, thank him for it, and render him all the glory of it. If it did not succeed, make to him an entire sacrifice of your will and desires, submitting yourself to his will, and judging that to be best which he ordains; which if you really do, you will gain more than if it had succeeded to your mind.

If you find yourself oppress'd with melancholy, or if any afflicting accident has happened to you, or any temptation, have recourse to Jesus, seek your solace and comfort in him alone, and tell him you expect help from no other.

Finally, in all your difficulties, have recourse to him.

Acts

Acts of Faith, Hope, Charity, spiritual Communion; and as before, after the first Visit.

SEC. IV.

On Monday the first Visit.

Go to Jesus in the Blessed Sacrament as to your Pastor. Consider the love he expresses for each of his flock, how he seeks to maintain their lives, and make them happy. He assures us that he loves us as his Father loves him. Ask him, but ask it from your heart, that you and all the community may for ever be of the number of his sheep.

Grant, dear Lord, this favour, since I am sure you desire it; content then this your desire by granting it. It is what I confide, and hope you will; and let not the force of our common enemy take any of us out of your hands. Reform, dear Lord, the deformity of my soul, and no longer suffer any thing to remain in me that displeases you. Employ me according to your merciful designs over me, and give me the grace promptly to conform

form myself to them, and to sanctify myself, and those that are under my charge, by perfectly fulfilling all the duties of my employment, to the greater glory of your name.

Inspire me with those sentiments of love and tenderness for each, which may resemble that you have for them; that after having laboured with you on earth for their Salvation, I may, for recompence, enjoy you for ever in heaven. Amen.

Acts of Faith, Hope, Charity, as before.

The second Visit on the same Day in the Spirit of Zeal.

Your Sacred heart, dear Jesus, in this adorable Sacrament, burns with an inexplicable love for all men; and therefore I am persuaded that I cannot please you more, than in petitioning you in favour of miserable sinners, whom your enemy holds under the Captivity of sin, and in imploring your mercy for Hereticks ignorant of our faith. Remember, Lord, that they are the work of your hands, and created to your image and likeness.

likeness. Hell is filled with them to the dishonour of your name, though you have shed your blood and died for their salvation. Dear Lord, let yourself be overcome by the Prayers of our Holy Mother the Church. Forget and forgive their sins and infidelities, and in satisfaction, receive all you suffered for them on the Cross. Grant them the spirit of penance, and grace to amend their lives, and to love and serve you the rest of their days.

I also petition your mercy in favour of the poor souls whom you love so tenderly, and so much desire their solace. They being detained in purgatory, are hindered from loving and glorifying you, as they would if they were in Heaven. It is on that account I beg their deliverance, and to obtain it I offer you all the merits of your Passion and Death, and the precious Blood you have shed for them, which I adore in this Divine Sacrament.

There is not a more efficacious means to partake of God's liberalities than to press him for our neighbour, whether living or dead; so charitable a proceeding opens the heart and hand of God, to replenish us with his graces and blessings.

Acts

Acts of Faith, Hope, and Charity, as above.

Third Visit as above also.

SEC. III.

Tuesday—First Visit.

'Go to Jesus in the Blessed Sacrament, as to your Judge. Tell him the terror you have of being judged, not knowing whether you are worthy of his love or hatred; not being certain if you love him as he requires of you. But tell him, if to be of the number of his friends, it is sufficient truly to desire to be so, you have some reason to hope you are, since you really desire to love him above all things.

But, dear Lord, whether my heart will remain constant to your love, to my last breath, is what I am not certain of; the uncertainty of which makes me tremble. It is you only that can give me that assurance, by giving me such a love that no waters of tribulation may extinguish.

It is to obtain that favour of your mercies that I approach your Holy Altar, which

which is properly the tribunal of those mercies, thereby to be enabled to appear with assurance before the tribunal of your justice. Here in place of bidding me retire, you ordain me to approach, saying, *Come to me all you that are burdened with the heavy weight of your sins, and I will ease and refresh you.*

Acts of Faith, &c. as above.

*Second Visit for the same Day.
In the Spirit of Love.*

Go to Jesus in the Blessed Sacrament to express your love to him, for the many marks he gives you of his, especially this of remaining for ever with you. Beg him to inspire you with sentiments of his love, worthy of himself. If you find your heart so dry that you cannot make such an act of love as you wish to do, offer him all the love with which he is loved by all the Blessed of Heaven.

It will be time well spent if you employ yourself in begging of him the grace to love him and his eternal Father perfectly in this life, and eternally in the next. But ask it with an entire confidence,

dence, not doubting to experience the truth of his words, who assures us that if we ask we shall receive.

Grant then, dear Jesus, that I may love you in this Sacrament, as much as I am beloved by you. Be wholly yours, as you are wholly mine. Hear my Prayers—pity my Sighs—hearken to my Petition. You command me to love you. Alas! you know my weakness and incapacity to do it as I ought. Give then what you command, and command what you please. Employ your omnipotent hand to destroy whatever opposes it in me, as self-love, which I beg you to annihilate in me, that your love alone may reign in my heart.

Acts of Faith, Hope, &c. as above.

Third Visit as before.

SEC. VI.

Wednesday—First Visit.

Go to Jesus in the Blessed Sacrament as to your Lord and Sovereign, whose power is infinite, he can with all imaginable

nable ease do whatever he will, for to *will* and to *do* is the same thing with God. Rejoice thereat, and that his goodness is equal to his power.

Dear Lord, what comfort for my poor soul, which you seem to have created so miserable, only that you might have the satisfaction to draw me out of it, and to shew your mercy to me. Behold then all my miseries and necessities; see how I am surrounded with enemies without and within, by my Passions and vicious inclinations which tyrannise over me. Behold sufficient matter both for your power and mercy to work upon; for no less a power than yours can change me from what I am to what I ought to be; nor can a less mercy will it: Say but the word, and I shall be victorious, and for ever happy.

Acts of Faith, Hope, &c. as above.

The second Visit for the same Day.

By way of amorous Complaints.

How comes it, dear Lord, since you are so merciful as to remain constantly on our Altar to do me good, that I am still what

what I am, poor, and in want of all things? It must be that I know not how to make use of so powerful a means as I have in you; for in you is contained a remedy for all my evils. You are that Physician whose power and skill cures all diseases. If then I am still sick and wounded, the fault must be my own, since you are willing to cure me. Teach me, dear Lord, where it lies, that knowing it I may correct it.

It is not that I am ignorant of your love and tenderness for me, and consequently have but small confidence in you, though you remain for ever here that I may find in you a powerful Protector, a Father, a Physician, and the best of friends. Make me then know you better that I may love you more; for to love you but little is not to know you; and knowing you, may I confide in you, and make recourse to you in all my necessities.

Acts

Acts of Faith, Hope, &c. as above.
Third Visit as above also.

SEC. VII.

Thursday—First Visit.

Go to Jesus in the Blessed Sacrament, as to the Soul's Food in life, and viaticum at death. This Divine Food comes from Heaven, and will conduct us thither.

Good God, is it possible that the recompence of Saints, the joy of Angels, the Eternal Word should make himself the Food and Nourishment of my soul! What can I desire more? Nothing, dear Lord, but that I may correspond with such a love, and ever worthily dispose myself to receive you, until I happily arrive to you, for the strength of this Divine Sacrament can make me walk in the way of perfection during life, and open to me the gate of Heaven at my death.

Grant, dear Lord, that your presence in this adorable Sacrament, at the hour of my death, may dissipate all fears which the enemy and my sins may then cause in me, and give me due dispositions to receive

ceive my viaticum with an humble and assured confidence in your goodness and mercy; and in the promise you make me, that if I eat your flesh, and drink your blood, I shall live for ever. Let your goodness in then visiting me give me a fresh assurance of it, and make me leave this world with joy and comfort.

Acts of Faith, Hope, &c. as above.

Second Visit for the same Day, in the Spirit of Gratitude.

Reflect that Christ descends from Heaven to earth expresly for your sake alone, as often as you communicate, foreseeing that in such an host (into which he enters) you will receive him: This he does with a design to sanctify you, and to enrich you with his graces, being in that host only for you, and there he prays and offers himself to his Eternal Father for you; and his heart burns with love for you, and with a desire of inflaming yours.

Dear Saviour, what obligation have I to you! and how can I sufficiently thank you for being thus pleased to think on me, and to work such wonders for my sake?

fake? I offer you in return all the thanks that are rendered you by the Blessed in Heaven, and by your servants on earth. What can I wish for more than you have done? Nothing, but that you would please to bid me come to you, for knowing myself unworthy, I dare not otherways approach. And this you also do, saying, *Come to me all you that are burdened, and I will refresh and ease you.* This being, I will not fear to approach and receive you, since I have your orders for it.

Whilst I may thus approach to you and receive you in this Divine Sacrament, no loss shall afflict me; for in you I have all that is, or can be necessary for me. Grant I may, in some sort, merit this effect of your love, by suffering and labouring for your glory in this adorable Mystery. And since your food in it is the virtues of our souls, and the love and honour we pay you, when we receive you, my chief care shall be to prepare my soul for that happiness.

Acts of Faith, Hope, &c. as above.

Third Visit as above also.

SEC. VIII.

Friday—First Visit.

Go to Jesus in the Blessed Sacrament as to your soul's Lover. His love for us is unmeasurable, remaining continually with us, desiring to communicate his benefits, and unite himself entirely to us. A life of thirty-three years spent for our service seems too short to him, and therefore he works the greatest of miracles, to satisfy the greatest of desires. He is pleased to say, his delights are to be with the children of men, and he makes it appear in this adorable Mystery.

My dear Redeemer, is it possible that you should love me, your unworthy creature, to such an excess, as to give yourself wholly to me? Have you then forgot my offences, and the ill treatment you have received from me, when so good as to visit me? You hate sin infinitely, yet you hate it less than you love me. O Divine

Divine heart of my Saviour, worthy the love of all hearts! I consecrate mine to you; fill it with your love, that so it may be worthy of your acceptance, and let your heart be touched with my miseries, the greatest of which is, that I so little love what is so infinitely amiable. But since you desire to unite yourself to me, unworthy as I am, by this heavenly Mystery, which is a Mystery of union, effect it to your glory.

Acts of Faith, Hope, &c. as above.

The second Visit on the same Day, in the Spirit of Praise.

O my sovereign Lord, it is impossible for me to praise you as I ought, for that incomparable love you express for me in this Divine Sacrament, making yourself my food and nourishment in this life, and my recompence in the next. And for all the graces and favours you have done me, and are continually ready to bestow upon me; therefore to supply for my inability, I offer you, in return, all the praises that have been, are, and will be rendered you for all eternity.

Blessed

Blessed Angels and happy Saints, I most humbly beg you to praise, bless, and glorify my Sovereign and yours in my behalf. Give him, I beseech you, the honour I ought to pay to his Divine Majesty; and I, with my whole heart, join and unite my intention to all the love, adorations, and glory you shall ever give him for a whole eternity.

Then remain in silence, admiring his Perfections and the Prodigies of his Love exprest in this Sacrament. For one of his Prophets speaking to him says, *Silence, my God, is one of the things that praises you most loudly.*

Acts of Faith, Hope, &c. as above.

Third Visit as above also.

SEC. IX.

Saturday—First Visit.

Go to Jesus in the Blessed Sacrament, as to your Master, humbly beg him to teach you all that is necessary for you to know, or that he would have you to learn.

Great

Great God, grant this favour to your poor creature, speak to my heart in this visit, and teach me all you would have me do. For I should make more profit in perfection, if, in place of others, you would speak to me yourself; for that is soon learnt which you teach. Speak then, dear Lord, and teach me all that belongs to my duty and charge: make me learn to do it well; for you only can give sense and understanding to your scholars. Make me not only learn, but retain whatever you shall teach me, that so I may faithfully practise it.

And since you are pleased to remain continually with me, I will, before I go to others, come to you for instructions. But if, Divine Master, I am not quick at learning, or forget what I have learned, pardon and pity my weakness, and have patience with me.

Acts of Faith, &c. as above.

The second Visit for the same Day.

In the Spirit of Poverty and Want.

Christ, in the Blessed Sacrament, is infinitely rich, wise, and powerful. If, as Holy

Holy Scripture tells us, the Queen of Saba went from the extremities of the earth to see the riches, and hear the wisdom of Solomon; and if he gave her all she *would* and *asked*, besides what he, out of his Royal Munificence, presented her; What may you hope for? make your reflections upon all this, and confide the like will be your lot. With his riches he will enrich you; with his wisdom he will enlighten you, solve your doubts, and clear your difficulties; and with his strength he will defend and fortify you against your enemies.

Say to his Divine Majesty, Lord, behold here a miserable Creature, indigent and beggarly, and an object of pity. The least sign from you will make me happy, and you will lose nothing by enriching me. Give me plenty then, for my wants are great, and I cannot be satisfied with a little; nor is it glorious to your name to give sparingly. Let your gifts be worthy of the giver. Bestow upon me your love, your grace, your fear, and a zeal of your glory, and of the Sanctification of my Soul. It will redound more to your glory to enrich me with these gifts, thereby to
save

save me, than to ruin me by the refusal of them.

Acts of Faith, Hope, Charity, as above.

The third Visit as above also.

Besides three Visits each day, you cannot do less to comply with the persevering love of Jesus in the Blessed Sacrament, than to visit him from time to time as occasion will permit, though but for a moment, as at one time to adore him, another time to offer him your heart, and the hearts of all the community. Another time to beg his blessing for yourself and for those under your care. At other times to thank him for remaining continually with you. Then to beg he will make himself be as much beloved and honoured, in the adorable Sacrament in this house, as he is in any place upon earth.

In these sort of Prayers which we make in our Visits, and which are properly called aspirations, St. Francis, of Sales, would have us pronounce them rather with heart than with mouth; and he adds, that those which love suggests to us us upon the spot will be the best and most profitable.

CHAPTER IV.

Of the presence of God.

SEC. I.

How advantageous it is to keep ourselves in his presence.

THE exercise of the presence of God is the principal and most important of all other exercises of devotion. It is what gives life and motion to the rest, without which they will neither have force nor vigour.

It is that which makes the Just Man, guards the Just Man, and feeds the Just Man. There are but few that arrive to the perfection of this Holy Practice, because they meet with many difficulties which few have the courage to overcome. This exercise is the very root of all our spiritual good, by means thereof a soul becomes rich in grace and virtue.

It happens sometimes, that notwithstanding the desire we have of keeping
ourselves

ourselves in the simple view of God's presence, we find great tediousness and disgust in it; but this must not hinder us, for our motive in doing it ought to be purely to please God, and not to satisfy self-love, which would always find some relish or support, as well in exercises of Piety as in other things.

Peace is so necessary in order to this exercise, that we must always endeavour to keep our soul in peace, being ever upon our guard to admit of no disturbance, whatever happens to us, turning from all that may disquiet us as from a malignant vapour, and establishing ourselves in a firm and solid tranquillity, which makes us capable of all good, and without which we are capable of none.

Inquire Pacem & persequere eam. Seek Peace and follow it with great care.

In omnibus requiem quæsivi. I have sought peace in all things, and have endeavoured to possess an unshaken one in all events.

Summus sapientia finis est ut simus mente tranquilla. The end of wisdom is to keep our mind always in peace, and conserve ourselves in an inviolable tranquillity.

H   *Hæc*

Hæc est Vita consummati perfectique Sapientis. It is the life of the wise and perfect.

As peace is necessary in order to our keeping ourselves in the presence of God, so a lively faith of his presence and protection is the means to keep a soul in peace in the midst of troubles and pains. But we must understand that there are two sorts of peace; the one is accompanied with sweetness, in which case it is easy to be faithful to God, and practise virtue. But the other sort of peace is full of bitterness, interior pains and disgusts, which afflict a soul, notwithstanding she enjoys peace. This *Peace*, as holy Scripture calls it, is full of bitterness, and consists not in tasting the sweets of peace, but in suffering troubles, agitations, and interior pains, with an humble submission to the will of God; and this peace is incomparably more meritorious and sanctifying than the other. A soul agitated and tormented, without comfort from God or man, is sustained only by her Faith in God's presence, by which she keeps herself faithful to him in her duties, and submissive to his will; seeking purely to content him, without knowing
she

she does it. She is tormented by temptations, dryness, and disgusts in the exercises of Piety, so that she becomes a horror to herself, as thinking she is so to Almighty God, to whom in the mean time she is most pleasing; for by such trials he renders her more worthy of his love.

The presence of God is an habitual belief that God is present, and an elevation of our heart and mind to him by means of aspirations; the frequent use of which will both serve to keep us in his presence, and to bring us back again when we are strayed from it. These aspirations or ejaculatory Prayers are judged not only beneficial, but necessary to keep us from committing sin. They also comfort us in our afflictions; for the greatest consolation in this exile is to think of God, who is the source of all comfort. They render our actions supernatural, our days full of merit, and your lives worthy of God; making us live to God, of God, and continually in God's presence. And as his Divine Majesty has his Eyes always fixed on us, so the soul, by means of aspirations, turns her's towards him.

By the frequent ufe of this exercife we practife diverfe virtues, according to the diverfity of our afpirations. The fire of God's love is kindled and maintained in our hearts. The fpirit of devotion is acquired. It prevents fin from entering, or drives it out again, if entered. It gains the heart of God, and as it were ties him with a hair, that is, an aſſent of our thought.

As for the afpirations, they may be either what God then infpires us with, or what we have drawn from our morning meditation, or any that moves us moſt.

The times moſt neceſſary of ufing them are at the beginning, middle, and end of each action, and when the clock ſtrikes.

The interior occupation of a foul with God is a fpecial privilege of his grace, and depends on his mercy. It is not what we can attain to by any induſtry of ours. We muſt afk it of God by means of Prayer; for all our endeavours, without his help, will avail us nothing. We muſt daily beg of Almighty God that he will pleafe to grant us the grace frequently to remember his Divine prefence, and

and that with due dispositions of heart, an interior adoration and tender affection.

Let us also beg our good Angels, who never lose sight of God, to mind us often of his presence, and obtain us the grace to increase thereby in his Holy Fear and Love.

SEC. II.

A Practice of the Presence of God, by means of Faith, Hope, and Charity, and Conformity to his Divine Will.

It is of very great importance to be persuaded that our perfection and happiness consists in the union of our souls, and its faculties, will, memory, and understanding, with God, by Faith, Hope, Charity, and Conformity to God's Will.

The most noble, profitable, and perfect action we can do in this life, or in the next, is to unite ourselves to God, and to his Divine Son Jesus Christ; because by this union (according to the Doctrine of the Saints) we become one Spirit with God. Now the most efficacious means we have of doing this, is by Faith, Hope, Charity, and Conformity to his Will; and therefore the practice of these

these virtues ought to be very familiar with us, and in a manner continual; or perhaps we may reap more advantage by taking one at a time for practice, and so change every month, beginning with the first in January, by which we shall have three separate months in a year for each of the four virtues.

SEC. III.

The Properties and Excellence of Faith.

Faith is the foundation, root, source, and measure of all other virtues; as much as we have of Faith, so much we shall have of Hope, of Charity, of Conformity to God's Will.

Faith is the virtue which is most pleasing and glorious to God, because it sacrifices the most noble faculty of our souls, to wit, the understanding. It is the most powerful of all other means to obtain what we desire, according to our Saviour's own words, *There is nothing impossible to them that have Faith.*

It is under the standard of Faith that all the other virtues rank themselves to fight their enemies. It is in that fortress they

they retire to defend themselves by a generous resistance against all the attacks of the enemy.

It is Faith that makes the just man prefer the service of God to any interest of his own. Without Faith, Charity cannot subsist, because Faith shews us how amiable God is, which makes us love him.

The blossom that precedes the fruit, and the foundation which supports the whole Edifice of all the other virtues.

SEC. IV.

The Practice of Faith.

1st, We must believe with a pure, blind, and naked Faith, all the mysteries of our Holy Religion, and the truths, speculative and practical, revealed by God.

2dly, We must believe them incomparably more than all that appears evident in nature.

3dly, And although the world should doubt, yet we should resolve to live and die in that belief.

Then

Then we muſt deſcend to ſome particulars. One of the moſt important is, the preſence of God in all places. His providence over us, and care of us. For if we firmly believe that God looks on us, hearkens to us in all times and places, has a continual care and providence over us, continually thinks of us, and in all occaſions is attentive to our wants and neceſſities, and has a more than paternal affection to conduct us to our beatitude, it will breed in us an unſhaken confidence in God, and a tender filial love for him, and a high eſteem of his conduct, tho' never ſo contrary to the ſentiments of nature.

In omni loco oculi Domini contemplantur bonos & malos. The eyes of our Lord in all places contemplate the good and the bad.

Servavi mandata tua, & teſtimonia tua, quia omnes viæ meæ in ſonſpectu tuo. I kept your will becauſe I reflected that I was in your preſence, and that all my works were expoſed to your eyes.

Naked Faith is ſomething painful to beginners, becauſe the interior part and ſenſes have no ſhare therein, but ſeek to render ſenſible that which is ſpiritual, and
to

to reduce to experience that which belongs only to Faith. This is the weakness of our nature, which would fain feel things sensible. We must have patience with it; but not yield to it, but remain firm in the superior part of our souls by naked faith; firmly believing that God is present, though we have not any experience of it in ourselves; not so much as a good thought, nor any good sentiment, nor consolation, having in this no support but in Faith, by which we keep ourselves united to God present.

Thus raising ourselves above nature in the simple union of the Divine Presence, without seeing, relishing, or receiving any agreeable effects of it; content to believe God present, without seeking any other assurance, neither more light nor more consolation than he thinks fit; nor that he should manifest himself any other way than as he pleases.

The best means of keeping ourselves thus united to God, is that of aspirations, which we ought, at least, to make every half hour, or at farthest every hour. And though they are performed in a moment, their fruit is everlasting.

If

If we have not drawn any from our morning's Meditation, nor are not inspired by Almighty God with any particular one, we may make use of some one of the ensuing aspirations; and at the beginning and end of all our actions, adoring the Blessed Trinity present, refer it to the glory of the Divine Majesty, by the *Gloria Patri*, &c.

Upon both which we must make our particular examination, and be exact in marking down how often we have failed in the morning, and how often in the afternoon; for that will be a means to make us more faithful.

It must also be the virtue or fruit we draw from our Meditations; and we must heartily beg it of Almighty God in all our Prayers and Communions, the month that we pretend to make it our practice; being sensible that all endeavours will never obtain it unless he is pleased to give it to us.

Lastly, We must, once a Week, as long as we aim at making it our practice, read it over, and reflect for a quarter of an hour upon all that is here set down for that effect.

Some

Some proper Aspirations for this Intent.

My God, you always behold me, grant I may never cease to love you.

O my God, you are here present, grant me the grace never to offend you.

God of my heart, make me what you would have me.

Great God, draw my heart entirely to you.

God of goodness, have mercy on me. My God, save your poor creature; let not my soul be lost which has cost you so dear.

Lord, make me perfectly love you, and always obey you.

My God, your goodness is infinite, and the love with which you love me is from eternity! You are my portion and my inheritance. I desire nothing besides you.

SEC. IV.

The way of keeping ourselves united to God, by the virtue of Hope.

This virtue makes us hope in God, and of God the possession of all good, and

and a deliverance from all evils, both those of this life and of the next; this hope is founded on his goodness, the fidelity of his promises, and the merits of Christ. As this virtue has regard to God alone, from whom we expect succours and remedy to all our necessities, it is pure and naked, and shutting our eyes to all that weakens it, whether from ourselves or from creatures, it may be called blind.

The Properties and Excellence of Hope.

First, It is very pleasing to Almighty God, and does truly honour him; because it purely proceeds from the great esteem we have of his goodness.

It procures immense treasures; for it obtains of God all that it asks, and gives courage to overcome difficulties, because it leans upon the power of God, and confers on our souls an eminent perfection.

It creates in us a great confidence in the Divine Majesty, whom we believe present, which thought raises our dejected Spirits, and inspires joy. It is all the consolation we have in our exile.
What

What should we do in this World, if we did not think of the God of comfort and Father of mercies? as such he is moved with our miseries. He knows the state we are in, and what troubles us; and can and will help us, if, considering him present, we make recourse to him with confidence. My God, says our Holy Father, *You love me too much to abandon me. It is sufficient that you know my necessities, to convince me that you will do whatever is best for your Glory and my good.*

Non timebo mala quoniam tu mecum es: I will not fear the evils which surround me, because you are with me to sustain and deliver me.

Quoniam in me speravit liberabo eum; protegam eum quoniam cognovit Nomen meum. I will deliver him and protect him, because he knows my Name; that is to say, because he looks on me, and honours me as his Father. He shall have recourse to me, and I will hear him. I will be with him in his tribulations, and deliver him.

You men of little Faith, said our Lord, Why do you doubt, since I am with you. This he said to his Apostles, and the

I same

same he says to each of us, being present *every* where. Fear nothing but to confide in my goodness, for nothing can hurt you as long as you confide in me. What a comfortable assurance!

The Practice of Hope.

1st, We must firmly hope that God will give us all that he has promised us. And this we must hope with a pure, naked, and blind Hope.

2dly, We must hope it with an unshaken firmness, incomparably more than we hope for any thing from any creature, whatever affection they may have for us.

3dly, Though all mankind should doubt, yet with God's grace we would live and die in that persuasion and hope.

Then we must descend to some particulars, as that God will have care of our Life and Death, and will assist us in our Temptations, Afflictions, and Maladies; and that he will dispose of us, and of all that relates to us, as he sees best for his glory and our good.

Proper

Proper Aspirations for this Intent.

Tu es, Domine, spes mea. You are, O Lord, my only Hope.

In Verbum tuum superspreravi. In your word I have hoped above all.

Etiam si occiderit me, in ipso sperabo, & ipse erit Salvator meus. Although you should afflict me with all evils, and should kill me, yet I will not cease to hope in you, my God and Saviour.

Non timebo mala quoniam tu mecum es. I will fear no evil, because you, Lord, are with me.

Dominus regit me & nihil mihi deerit; our Lord governs me and has care of me, and nothing shall be wanting to me.

And with St. Francis, when he floated upon a plank in the sea,

What have I to fear, God sees me, and can help me? I will whatever he pleases.

The better to keep ourselves united to God present, by means of hope, we may use some of these aspirations, or the like, every half hour, or at least every hour; and at the beginning of each action, being sensible that we stand in need of God's Assistance and Help. Let us beg it with confidence by those words, *Deus in adjutorium,* &c. on both which we must make our particular examen as above.

We must also make that virtue our chief aim in our Meditations, and the fruit we draw from them, during the time we take it for practice; begging it of Almighty God, in all our Prayers and Communions, as being sensible that all our labours and endeavours will avail us nothing, unless God is pleased to bestow it on us.

Lastly, We must, once a week, as long as we aim at the practice of this virtue, take a quarter of an hour to read over and reflect upon what is here set down for that effect.

SEC. VI.

How to keep ourselves united to Almighty God, by the Means of Charity.

It is the virtue which makes us love God and ourselves, and all things else for him, without mixture of our own interest, or that of any creature, by which our Charity is pure, naked, and blind, shutting our eyes to all things but God.

We

We have certainly an infinity of motives to love God; but laying them aside, the tender name of Father ought to suffice, it being a name of pure love, which expresses the love he bears us, and also marks the love we owe and ought to pay him.

The Properties and Excellence of Charity.

Charity is the virtue which gives worth to all we do. It is not counsel, but a command made by God. It is the first, the greatest, and the most sweet of all his commands, as well as the most necessary. If we love him not, having so many obligations to do it, we are the basest of his creatures, and unworthy of such a command.

Charity, without dispute, is the greatest of all virtues. It is the very soul and life of them, and renders them worthy of eternal beatitude. It is the accomplishment of God's law. It procures most honour to his Divine Majesty, and most merit to ourselves. It gives force to do and suffer great things for his service.

The Practice of Charity.

1st, To love God, ourselves, and all things else for him, with a pure, naked, and blind Charity.

2dly, To resolve to live and die in his love, though thereby we should incur all evils.

3dly, To perform all we do for the love of God, which is to walk with large steps to Perfection and true Sanctity.

4thly, To obey the Divine Majesty in all things, especially in loving our neighbour, because he will have it so; and doing them all the good we can, because he will take to himself whatever we do to them.

Aspirations proper for this Intent.

O God, of love, reign in my heart, and possess it alone.

My God I love you above all things; but if I love you not enough, grant I may love you more.

Give me that love you command, and then command what you please.

Come,

Come, Lord, and reign in the midst of your enemies, and destroy all that opposes your love in me.

Great God, you fill Heaven and earth; let not my heart be void and empty of your love.

Dear Lord, grant me a holy hatred of myself, and a perfect love of you.

You are my God, and that contents me. My God and my all.

These aspirations will serve both to enkindle the love of God in our hearts, and to maintain and keep it alive. We must, therefore, frequently use them, as every half hour, or at least every hour; and at the beginning of each action, considering God's benefits to us in that action, (the more to inflame our hearts with love) thanking him for the same with these words, *Deo gratias*, performing it for love of him, saying, *propter te.*

Upon both these specified times for aspirations, we must make our particular examen, and not forget a weekly reflection, as mentioned after the other two virtues, Faith and Hope.

SEC.

SEC. VII.

Of Conformity to God's Will, and the Manner of keeping ourselves united to God present, by Means of the same.

The Will of God must, of necessity, tend to his Glory, and our Salvation and Sanctification. We must then conclude that the most natural and efficacious means to glorify God and to sanctify ourselves, is to accomplish his Will. We have nothing properly our own but our will. When we strip ourselves of it, we then possess nothing, by which we are put in a capacity of being filled with God.

The Will of God is signified to us by the orders of his Providence. For it is an Article of Faith that God knows all and disposes of all; and that nothing happens but by the orders of his Providence, and by the disposition of his Will. We must then submit ourselves to them, both as to what concerns ourselves and others, and to all the accidents of this life. And believe it the duty of our will in point of obedience to God's Will, as
it

it is of our understanding in Point of Faith, to renounce all human reason.

The Properties and Excellence of Conformity to God's Will.

Conformity to the Divine Will is the noblest of all other employments, having for object the highest End, which is the Will of God. It is the shortest way to perfection, and the most efficacious means to solid peace of mind.

It is what in some manner we are obliged to, since it is impossible that God should not desire, and even exact that his Will and good Pleasure should be the universal rule of all the actions of his creatures. It is the most profitable manner of the Presence of God; by it we walk with God, and are conducted by him as sheep by their Pastor, even to the mount of Perfection.

By it we become Victims of God. The perpetual resignation of ourselves into the hands of God, in all events submitting to his will, and accepting all the effects of his providence, is one of the most essential and most advantageous practices of a spiritual life, producing in them

them that use it, peace, purity of heart, and Divine love, more than all other practices.

By it we exercise not an ordinary charity towards God, but an effective love. We may lawfully rest content with this practice, which will supply the place of Man's Devotions.

Vita in Voluntate ejus. Life and all sorts of good are found in the accomplishment of God's Will.

The Practice.

First, To beg Almighty God to establish in our souls a perfect submission to all his wills.

2dly, To make acts of conformity to his blessed will, in all that relates to us, both in body and soul, goods, honours, pleasures, time, and eternity; and also in all that God permits to happen amongst creatures in heaven, earth, and hell; in nature, grace, and glory; desiring that all should be as God would have it.

3dly, When we find pain and difficulty to obey God, and feel motions of revolt against his designs and dispositions over us, to say with David, *My soul, will you*

you not submit to God? Will you be rebellious to him from whom you have received all you have, and are?

Obmetui & non aperui es meum quoniam tu fecisti. I held my peace that I might not say a word against what happened, because it was you that permitted it.

Aspirations proper to keep us united to God's Will.

Lord, I accept with submission of all you ordain, both in regard of myself and others.

You are my Lord and Master, do what you please with me.

Ordain whatever you please, but give me grace to do whatever you ordain.

Make me according to your desire, always fulfilling your will.

Make me obey you perfectly.

Teach me to do your Will, because you are my God.

Come and reign in the midst of your enemies, and destroy all that opposes your Will.

Force my rebellious will to do yours for ever.

These,

These, or the like aspirations, if made every half hour, or at least every hour, will keep us united to God by conformity of our will to his. At the beginning of each Action, adoring God present and his Will, which calls us to that Action; let us say, my God, I do this to obey your Will; and I unite it to that obedience which my dear Saviour rendered to your Will; upon both these we must make our particular examen.

We must also make this virtue our chief aim in our Meditations, and the fruit we draw from them during the time we take it for practice: And beg it of Almighty God, in all our Prayers and Communions, being sensible that all our endeavours will avail us nothing in order to the attaining it, unless God gives it.

Every week we should observe these following things: 1st, For one quarter of an hour to read over and consider how we comport ourselves in the aforesaid practices of the presence of God; whether as set down for that effect; for constancy makes perfectness.

2dly, If those virtues produce the sentiments and effects proper, according to what

what is set down; for by the fruit we we must judge of the tree.

We should also, from time to time, examine whether we make use of the methods for hearing Holy Mass; if we read the motives before them, in order to raise in ourselves a high esteem and greater attention, by which we shall reap a far greater benefit from it. Then as to the Divine Office, mental Prayer, visits to the Blessed Sacrament, and beads; let us reflect how we perform them, whether according to the methods here proposed, or any other.

We should do well to write down the faults we find we have been guilty of, which will be a good means towards amendment.

An Oblation, or Profession of an entire Submission to God's Will, to be made from Time to Time.

My Lord and my God, I acknowledge the submission I owe to your Divine Will, which I cannot violate without offence. And that it is your will which governs and disposes of all things, either by an absolute ordinance, or a permissive one,

one, that a leaf cannot stir, nor a bird fly, nor a hair fall from our heads, without your permission. I acknowledge also that you created me purely to do your will. O pardon my having gone contrary to it, and give me grace to amend for the future, and to submit entirely to your will, in the manner that is most pleasing to your Divine Majesty.

I beseech you, dear Lord, through the merits of that perfect submission which my Saviour paid to all your wills, grant me the grace to have no will but yours, to which I abandon myself for life and death, time and eternity, and that I may rather chuse to die than deliberately desire any thing contrary to it. Grant I may, by conformity to your will, stifle in myself all contrary motions, that so your Divine Will may be victorious over mine.

It belongs to you, my God, to govern the world, and to bring each one to their end by the means you judge fit. We can chuse nothing better than what your wisdom ordains. It is our duty to let ourselves be conducted by you without diving into your councils, but humbly in all things submitting to your will, which

which I beg I may ever perform to your glory. *Amen.*

CHAPTER V.

SEC. I.

Motives of loving and honouring our Blessed Lady, and to raise a high Esteem for the Devotion of the Beads, which, of all others, is most acceptable to her.

FIRST, Our Lady is the Mother of God, and that alone ought to be a sufficient motive to render her all honour that may be given to a creature. She has none above her but God himself, and all that is not God is below her.

2dly, She is our Mother, given us by her Blessed Son, who gave us all to her on the cross, in the person of Saint John, and gave her to us all; so that we are equally with him her children, and she our Mother, and his will is that we both love and honour her, and make recourse to her as to a Mother.

3dly, Her love and charity for us, and desire of our good, infinitely surpasses that of all the Saints, as does her power to help us, being Mother to the Almighty.

4thly, No day of our lives should pass in which we do not render her the honour and duty we owe her, as to our most dear Mother, and Mother of our Redeemer. God comes to us by her, and by her intercession we may go to him. The most powerful helps of human misery are to be had by having recourse and devotion to our Lady.

Of all the Prayers in her honour we ought most to esteem the *Ave Maria*, which the oftner we say with devotion, the better. No Prayer ought to take place of it in our esteem, but the *Pater noster*, which is taught us by Christ himself, and therefore called his Prayer. It contains whatever he would have us ask, both for his glory and our good, and that in a few pathetic words. Which being, we cannot do better than to keep our mind and hearts occupied with the sense of the words, as we pronounce them, except prevented by some affection, as likely we may be, even with the first two words, *Pater noster*; when we reflect who it is we call Father, and that he assures us his love for us surpasses that of a Mother

ther to her Child, which, though she should forget, yet he would not forget us.

If this comfortable truth should take up our mind, we may rest there and go no further; for as long as we find ourselves so taken up, Saint Theresia says, it were to lose a great favour by our fault to do otherways, and that we do much more by saying some words after this manner, than by repeating the whole *Pater noster* several times without attention, or scarce knowing what we say.

The same Saint says, that some, to dispatch the task of Prayers they have set themselves, chuse rather to hurry them over, than to follow God's attract. In the Name of God, says the Saint, do not so, for you put an obstacle to the grace his Divine Majesty offers you, which is of great importance.

Let us say what we please of our beads, yet we must be convinced that all depends on being attentive to the words we speak, and united to the two objects of our Devotion, which are God and his Blessed Mother; otherways we shew that we have but little respect, when we chuse rather to be faithful to the number of our
Prayers

Prayers, (because we have a scruple to omit them) than to the well performance of them. For we do worse to say them so, than not to say them at all, except they were Prayers of Obligation, as the Divine Office, &c. And but hurrying over our others is not only a mispending our time, but also a singular disrespect to Almighty God.

After the *Pater noster*, no prayer ought to take place of the *Ave Maria*, which was composed, as you know, by the Angel, who had his orders from God, by Saint Elizabeth, inspired by the Holy Ghost, and by our Holy Mother the Church, moved by the same Spirit, to petition that powerful Lady in favour of her children; and therefore all that are so, ought to say it with great Devotion and attention.

In order to the better performance of this, we may make use of some one of these following methods, as shall be suitable with our present disposition. If we find difficulty in so many reflections for one *Ave Maria*, we may use but one at a time, and continue therein, not only during the whole *Ave Maria*, but the ten, and longer if we find our minds taken

ken up with it; and it will be more profitable than to change.

SEC. II.

A Method on the Words of the Angelical Salutation.

1. *Hail Mary,* Lady of this World, Queen of Heaven, whom all nations honour and worship.

2. *Hail Sea of Grief* in the Passion of your Son; for your grief was equal to your love, sufficient to have deprived you of life.

3. *Hail Mother of my Saviour,* in whom are all my Hopes.

1. *Full of Grace,* even from your Conception, then sanctified by the Holy Ghost, and built into a Temple fit to lodge the King of Angels.

2. *Full of Sanctifying Grace,* which in a far less measure makes other Saints.

3. *Full of Grace,* and to that fullness was added the fountain of all Grace, Christ our Saviour.

1. *Our Lord is with you,* not only as with his Saints and Servants, but in a
more

more excellent and high degree, being with you as your Son.

2. *Our Lord is with you,* in your understanding to enlighten it, and in your Will to inflame it above all others.

3. *Our Lord is with you* now in Heaven, and you with him in such a plenitude of Glory, that no creature else does, or ever shall enjoy the like.

1. *Blessed amongst Women,* interiorly in yourself, as being a Celestial Cabinet, in which is contained all the Blessings that you may obtain for us.

2. *Blessed amongst all on Earth,* as infinitely surpassing them all in greatness.

3. *Blessed amongst all* in Heaven, because seated above all, and nearer to God.

1. *Blessed is the Fruit of your Womb,* in himself essentially blessed from all eternity.

2. *Blessed is the Fruit of your Womb,* and so overflowing with the fullness of Blessings, that he made you blessed bearing him.

3. *Blessed is the Fruit of your Womb,* he being the Redeemer of sinners on the cross, and the Food of the Elect in the Blessed Sacrament.

2. *Jesus.*

2. *Jesus.* A Name of joy to Saints and Angels; a name of comfort and reverence to men; and a name of terror to the devils.

2. *Jesus.* A Name which illuminates when preached, feeds when thought on, and succours when invocated.

3. *Jesus.* A Name which confirms our joys, gives comfort in our grief, and hope in our despair.

1. *Holy Mary.* Who have the largest share of Holiness and Sanctity, as being not only free from sin, but also from all frailty in thought, word, or deed. All in you was virtuous, perfect, and holy.

2. *Holy Mary.* Holy above all the Saints the Church has produced, as reverencing the Divine Majesty with a more filial fear, loving him with a more inflamed charity, and soliciting his mercies for us with a more unwearied piety.

3. *Holy Mary.* As being the living Altar, consecrated to God, as being daughter to the eternal Father by adoption, Mother of the Son, Spouse of the Holy Ghost, and Sacred Temple of the Blessed Trinity.

1. *Mother of God,* and consequently the greatest of all creatures, and most Holy
of

of all Mothers, becaufe you conceived, by the Holy Ghoft, the fource of Holinefs.

2. *Mother of God.* Who is all goodnefs, all wifdom, and all mercy.

3. *Mother of God.* And therefore the moft glorious of Mothers, being Mother to him, who is Lord of Angels and King of glory.

1. *Pray for us Sinners,* to the Eternal Father, (whom we have much offended) that he will pleafe to pardon our fins, and write us in the book of life.

2. *Pray for us Sinners,* to Jefus your Son, and our Saviour, that he will apply to us the merits of his life and death, and pardon us our offences.

3. *Pray for us finners,* to God the Holy Ghoft, that he will replenifh our fouls with his fanctifying grace.

1. *Now,* Whilft we are yet upon our way to Eternity, encountering difficulties and temptations, and fighting our enemies.

2. *Now,* Whilft we live, and confequently offend or merit; the paft being out of our power, and the future not in it, therefore it is for the prefent we crave your help.

3. *Now,*

3. *Now*, This very moment, in this action, we beg your Prayers and affistance, which we ſtand in great need of, ſince obliged to fight againſt ourſelves.

1. *And at the hour of our death*, at that dreadful hour which opens the paſſage to Eternity. When whole armies of our ſins will appear before us in their horrid ſhapes, and our good works in a far ſmaller number, as we have reaſon to fear, ſtand unregarded by.

2. *At the hour of our death*, when we ſhall find nothing to hold us up, from ſinking into deſpair, but the mercies of God, and merits of our Saviour, to whom we beg your interceſſion.

3. *At the hour of our death*, when men will forſake us, and the Angels and Saints expect to ſee our paſſage and hear our doom. O Mother of mercy, at that hour open the bowels of your mercy to receive my laſt and deepeſt groans, that by your interceſſion making a happy end, I may praiſe and glorify the mercies of God, and thank your goodneſs for all Eternity.

SEC.

SEC. III.

A short Method on the Angelical Salutation.

1. At *Ave Maria*, to humble ourselves interiorly before her, whom God vouchsafed to honour above all others, by chusing her for his Mother, which renders her worthy of the greatest honour that men or Angels can render her.

2. *Gratia plena*, full of Grace, full even from her conception, fuller than all others. Happy plenitude, there being no vacancy for sin.

3. *Dominus Tecum, benedicta tu in Mulieribus*, &c. Our Lord is with her after a far different and more excellent manner, than with the rest of his servants, which causes admiration to the Angels; for he is with her not only as her God and Creator, but also as her Son and the fruit of her womb, which renders her the most blessed of all women.

4. *Sancta Maria.* Most Holy indeed, since in her dwelt the Holy of Holies.

5. *Ora pro nobis peccatoribus nunc.* Pray for all sinners, and particularly for me. Now at this very time, wherein I live, and

and consequently wherein I may offend; and all the remaining moments of my life, even till I arrive to eternity.

6. *Et in hora Mortis nostræ,* and at the hour of my death, which opens my passage to Eternity, I particularly beg your help and assistance then, and that you will shew yourself a Mother to me, so that if I am unprovided of human assistance, and suddenly called away, I may be helped by you, in whom next to the mercies of God, and merits of your Son, I put my total trust and Confidence. *Amen.*

At the end of every ten we must add the *Gloria Patri*, thanking the most blessed Trinity for all privileges and graces bestowed on our Lady; and at the end of our beads say a *Salve Regina* for a happy Death, and to beg her powerful assistance at that hour, lest we should then be incapable of doing it.

SEC. IV.

Another Manner of reciting our Beads.

In saying the three first Aves, we must honour our Lady as adopted Daughter of God

God the Father, Mother of God the Son, and Spouse of God the Holy Ghost.

The first ten is to be employed in acts of Faith—The second in acts of Hope—The third in acts of Love—The fourth in acts of Thanksgiving—The fifth in Petitions—And the sixth in Recommendations of ourselves. These acts may be applied to our Lady after this manner.

1st. Ten, acts of Faith that she is the most excellent, most holy, most powerful, most merciful, most wise, most perfect of all Creatures; and the worthy Queen of Angels and men, heaven and earth.

2d. Ten, of Hope as Mother of God, and most rich, merciful, and powerful, we hope she will obtain us the grace to live and die well, and never offend God mortally, to overcome our passions and all temptations, to fulfil our duties, and to arrive to the perfection God requires of us; all which we hope for through her intercession.

3d. Ten, of *Love*, exprest by her rejoicing that she is the Mother of God, Queen of Heaven and earth, and the most accomplished and perfectest of all

God's

God's works, praising and thanking God for it.

4th. Ten, of Thanksgiving for all benefits received from her, by her intercession, general and particular; and for her consenting to our dear Saviour's Death for our Salvation.

5th. Ten, of Petition for what we stand in need of, both for the corporal and spiritual; and not only for ourselves, but also for those we are obliged to pray for by duty, promise, or gratitude.

6th. Ten, to recommend ourselves to her Protection; begging her to shew herself a Mother to us, especially in obtaining for us whatever may render us more grateful and pleasing to God, as an ardent love of him, and great zeal to procure his honour and glory.

SEC. V.

A Method for saying the Rosary.

Offer the first five Tens in honour of the joyful Mysteries for those that are in mortal sin, or in any necessity, either spiritual or corporal.

In the first Ten address yourself to our Blessed Lady, as she is Daughter to the Eternal Father. Reflect on her singular Privileges. Congratulate with her for all the Prerogatives of joy and bliss she enjoys under that title. Give thanks for all favours received by her means.

At the end of each Ten add a *Gloria Patri* and the aspiration assigned.

Aspiration.

O Sacred Virgin, most dearly beloved Daughter of the Eternal Father, employ your credit and powerful intercession for all your Servants and Associates, who are unhappily fallen by sin from the right of Filiation, and are become children of Satan. Obtain them the grace of repentance, I beseech you. *Amen.*

Second Ten.

Consider our Blessed Lady as she is Mother of the Eternal Word. Make the same reflections as before.

Aspiration.

Aspiration.

Monstra te esse Matrem, shew yourself a Mother, especially to poor sinners. Obtain them mercy of your Blessed Son, and restoration of grace, by the merits of Christ's bleeding Wounds I beg it. *Amen.*

Third Ten.

Consider her as she is the Spouse of the Holy Ghost. Make the same reflections as before.

Aspiration.

Sacred Spouse of the Holy Ghost, obtain comfort for your desolate Servants and associates in their distresses, grace to rise from their tepid languors, and the love of God to inflame their hearts, O Mother of Divine love. *Amen.*

Fourth Ten.

Consider her as the Temple of the Blessed Trinity. Make the same reflections as before.

Aspiration

Aspiration.

O Sacred Temple of the living God! restore by your Intercession this title to your servants, who by sin have lost it. Obtain strength for them that are tempted to forfeit it; and never permit them to become slaves of the devil by transgressing the laws of God. *Amen.*

Fifth Ten.

Consider her as Queen of Angels and men. Reflections as before.

Aspirations.

O Sacred Queen, cast a favourable eye upon your poor subjects here on earth, especially those who have devoted themselves to your service in this Association of the Rosary; but above all, have compassion on all such as are in mortal sin, or in any affliction, corporal or spiritual. *Amen.*

The Second Five Tens in honour of the sorrowful Mysteries, for all the Associates that are agonizing.

Consider five of the chief virtues most resplendent in our Lady's life, making Acts of Love, Complacence, and Admiration.

First Ten.

Reflect on her ardent Love, and raise in yourself the aforesaid Affections.

Aspiration.

O Mother of beautiful love, if ever you obtained any sparks of that Divine Fire for any of your suppliants, we now humbly beg that favour for all your Associates now agonizing, that they may happily die in love, to live eternally. *Amen.*

Second Ten.

Consider her profound humility as before.

Aspiration.

O Sacred Virgin, Mother and Mistress of the Humble, succour now your children agonizing, and ending the course of this mortal Pilgrimage. Obtain them a profound Humility, that they may attain to Eternal Life. *Amen.*

Third Ten.

Consider her Virginal Purity of body and soul. Affections as before.

Aspiration.

O Virgin of Virgins, have compassion on the souls of your agonizing Servants, who are terrified with the apprehensions of past sins and offences, wherewith they have unhappily defiled the purity of their souls. Obtain them true Contrition and Eternal Life. *Amen.*

Fourth Ten.

Consider her firm Hope and Confidence in God. Affections as before.

Aspiration.

Aspiration.

O Mother of the Desolate, obtain a firm Hope and Confidence in the mercies of God for all the Agonizing of this Confraternity. Take from them all diffidence, and obtain their Eternal Salvation. Amen.

Fifth Ten.

Consider her heroic patience. Affections as before.

Aspiration.

O Mother of the Miserable, beg comfort for your afflicted agonizing servants! obtain them true patience in their sufferings, and a happy passage to eternal joy. Amen.

The Third Five Tens, in honour of the Glorious Mysteries, and for all the Associates detained in Purgatory.

Give thanks to our Blessed Lady for all Benefits received from her, by her intercession.

First Ten.

Look on her as your Mother, and give thanks for all her tender love, and Motherly care of you and the rest of the Associates.

Aspiration.

Dearest Mother, shew yourself the Mother of mercy to the souls of your Associates suffering in Purgatory. Look on them as your children. Let your mercies be to them a heavenly dew to mitigate their flames. *Amen.*

Second Ten.

Look on the Blessed Virgin as your Lady and Mistress. Give thanks for all favours received from her under that title. Look on yourself as her servant and handmaid.

Aspiration.

O dearest Lady, employ your credit with your Son, for your suffering servants in Purgatory. Cover and hide their faults under the mantle of your charity. *Amen.*

Third Ten.

Look on the Blessed Virgin as your Protectress, and give thanks for all favours of that nature.

Aspiration.

O Sacred Virgin, our refuge, cast a favourable eye on your afflicted clients in Purgatory. Appease the Divine Justice in their behalf. Present these our small devotions offered for them, and pray they may be effectual for their succour. *Amen.*

Fourth Ten.

Look on the Blessed Virgin as your Advocate; give thanks for all favours obtained in that kind.

Aspiration.

O Sacred Virgin, prove now a powerful Advocate for the poor souls of this Confraternity suffering in Purgatory. Obtain their speedy deliverance. *Amen.*

Fifth

Fifth Ten.

Look on the Blessed Virgin as a dear and confident friend. Give thanks for all favours in that kind.

Aspiration.

O Sacred Virgin, offer these Prayers to your Blessed Son, for your friends and servants suffering in Purgatory. Pray they may be effectual for some of their deliverance. *Amen.*

CHAP. VI.

SEC. I.

A Practice of Devotion to our Angel Guardian.

TAKE one day of each month to honour your good Angel. As for example: The second Sunday in the month confess and communicate in his honour; and after having employed one quarter after Communion in thanksgiving for the said favour, reflect upon the great goodness

goodness of that God you possess within you, who, knowing your weakness, and the danger you are exposed to both for soul and body, and the difficulty you have to defend yourself against your enemies, has appointed you one of his Angels, who are the Princes of his heavenly court, and has given him orders to assist and defend you, and never to leave you as long as your soul is in your body.

Return his Divine Majesty most humble thanks for so infinite a favour, and admire the value he puts on your soul, and the love he has for it, since he thus employs an Angel for your service. Then with great respect and humility address yourself to your Angel Guardian and Keeper, thank him for accepting the charge of you, and since, on his part, he promises you four things, and faithfully performs them: Do you the like, and be as faithful in your performance as he is.

First, he promises you to be ever present, and never to abandon you.

2dly, To cherish and love you as a child of God, bought with his Blood, and designed for the same glory he enjoys.

3dly, To guard both your body and your soul, and to procure what is best for both.

4thly, To continue his care of you in all times and places, till your soul is separated from your body.

On your part, promise him also four things, and beg his assistance for the performance.

First, A great reverence and respect to him, and neither to think, say, or do any thing deliberately that may offend or displease him.

2dly, A great love and tender devotion to him, loving him as your Father and best of friends, and endeavouring to increase his glory and joy in heaven, by the Holiness of your life upon earth.

3dly, A great confidence in his care and protection over you, and to have recourse to him as a child to the arms of its Mother in all your pains and difficulties, invocating his help in all.

4thly, To persevere in these duties till your last breath.

This Contract being made between your good Angel and you, beg our dear Lord, whom you have received, to bestow his Benediction upon it. Then retire in company of your good Angel, and from time to time entertain yourself with him the rest of the day. Sometimes thanking

thanking him for all the good turns he has done you from the day of your birth (which was the day he firſt began to take care of you) till this preſent moment, reflecting on the chief, and, next to God, attributing them to him.

Sometimes aſking his pardon for having paſſed ſo many years of your life without thinking of him, or at leaſt very little. And for having ſo often contriſtated him by your imperfections, and ſo ſeldom made your recourſe to him in your neceſſities, or thanked him for his benefits.

At other times open your heart to him, declare to him your neceſſities, and beg him to ſolicit God in your behalf. Deſire him to give you light in your doubts, help in your dangers, comfort in your afflictions, and Victory over your Enemies, with his particular aſſiſtance at the hour of your death.

Moreover, during the day, addreſs yourſelf to him by ſhort aſpirations, and if time will permit you, perform ſome Devotion in his honour, as his Office, or Litanies, or ſome Colloquies, &c.

CHAPTER VII.

Of Confession.

SEC. I.

Of Spiritual Confession.

AS there are two sorts of Communion; the one Spiritual, the other Sacramental; so there are two sorts of Confession, the Spiritual and the Sacramental. The one is made to Almighty God in the ear of a Priest, and the other to God alone, accusing ourselves in his presence of all we think we have offended him in; and exciting ourselves to the same affections of sorrow, hatred, and purpose of amendment, as when we confess Sacramentally.

This sort of Confession is very profitable and useful, and is the best disposition for Sacramental Confession, and as spiritual Communion supplies for the Sacramental, so does spiritual Confession for Sacramental Confession.

By practising this, we shall acquire a greater purity of soul, and the oftener we we perform it, the more will our souls be washed and cleansed from our sins, and become more beautiful in the sight of God; and if Death should surprise us, so that we could not confess Sacramentally, this might suffice to save us.

Whenever we make this Spiritual Confession, we must place ourselves in spirit at the feet of Christ Crucified, beholding the several Wounds our sins have caused him.

Then beg light to see and understand our sins; after which we must accuse ourselves of them, and when we accuse ourselves of the greatest, we must do it with a particular sentiment of humility and penance.

Contrition is the principal part both of Spiritual and Sacramental Confession, and ought to be rather interior motions of the soul, than exterior words. It consists in being heartily sorry for having offended so good a God. To excite us to it, we may reflect on that which follows; but are not obliged to make use of all, one may suffice, according as we find ourselves moved.

First, I who have offended God, am not only a Christian, but a Religious person,

sion, prevented, and obliged by so many benefits, eating the bread of his house, and esteemed for his Child, Spouse, and Servant.

2dly, By sinning, I have preferred a bawble, a thing of no consequence, before Almighty God, and this whilst he has the goodness to sustain and support me, and whilst I actually enjoy his benefits.

3dly, The little respect for his presence, sinning before his Divine Majesty, and dishonouring our Saviour's Passion.

4thly, The number of times, which surpasses the hairs of my head.

Having excited in our souls a true sorrow, and resolution never more to offend deliberately, though there were contained in any sin all the honours, riches, and pleasures that have been, or ever will be in the world; or that we should know for certain, that after having offended, we should neither have remorse of conscience, nor be punished in this world nor the next, and should, by sinning, avoid pain or confusion; yet for the Love of God we would not offend him. Then, with Humility and Sorrow, let us beg Pardon of his Divine Majesty, saying,

Dear

Dear Lord, if ever you shewed yourself a God of mercy, now is the time to appear so; for behold in your presence a monster of ingratitude, after all you have done to purchase my Salvation.

If heaven was amazed at the sight of a God crucified and dying, behold a new subject of amazement, and excess of goodness on the one side, and of ingratitude on the other. So much sufferings and Blood, such precious Blood shed for me, which by my offences I have trampled under foot, yet I hope for pardon; for it was never heard since the world had a being, that a sinner with sorrow asked your pardon and was refused. Your word stands engaged for it, that at what hour soever a sinner shall be truly sorry, you will pardon him. Dear Lord, either blot this out of your Book, or pardon and forgive me now.

SEC. II.

Of Sacramental Confession.

As the benefit of the Sacraments is the greatest help we have in this life, so on the good and frequent use of them, depends

pends not only our pefection but Salvation alſo; for thereby we receive increaſe of grace and ſtrength to amend our lives; and the merits of Chriſt are applied to us as often as we frequent them. But this in proportion to the diſpoſitions we bring.

By Confeſſion we are delivered from the greateſt of evils, which is ſin. Frequent confeſſion is a perpetual application of the benefit of our Redemption, which blots out our paſt ſins, and gives us ſtrength to avoid them for the future.

Nothing conduces more to our Salvation and perfection, than often frequenting the Sacrament of Penance; becauſe, by the reiterated application of the Blood of Chriſt, our hearts are more diſengaged and purified from ſin; for it not only blots out the paſt, but gives us grace and ſtrength to avoid committing new ones, and maintains in us the ſpirit of Penance, which is ſo pleaſing to God, and ſo neceſſary for Salvation.

The requiſite diſpoſitions to receive the benefit of the Sacraments, are Humility and Purity of intention, which muſt be to pleaſe God, and to unite ourſelves to him.

To make a good Confession, depends not so much on having a good Memory and a good Tongue, as on the having a good Heart, a good Will, a sincere detestation of our sins, and a firm resolution to correct them.

We ought ever to go to Confession as if it were to gain a jubilee, looking on it as the application of Christ's blood to our souls for the Remission of our sins and increase of grace. We should endeavour to go to it with the same dispositions as to communion.

Prayers before examen of Conscience.

I render you infinite thanks, dear Lord, for having instituted this Sacrament of Penance, by means of which I may obtain pardon of all my sins, and re-enter into favour and friendship with you; nay, even become still more united to you. Dear Lord, give those dispositions to my soul, which may, by means of this Sacrament, effect this to your greater Glory.

Divine Spirit, by the Sacred Wounds of Jesus, I beg light to see and know my sins, and the grace to be truly sorry for them,

them, and to confess them with due dispositions.

Mother of mercy and refuge of sinners, obtain me the grace so to approach this Sacrament, that I may by it be cleansed and purified of all sins.

O Holy Angel my Guardian, you have been witness of all I have done amiss, remind me of my offences, help me to confess them as I ought, and beg pardon of Almighty God for me.

O my God, since on the Sanctity of my Confession depends my perfection and eternal Salvation, and that I cannot perform them as I ought, but by the assistance of your grace; give me that light necessary to know my sins, and that Humility with which I ought to confess them. Give me also your love, that I may have a perfect Contrition for them and your grace, that for the future I may avoid them.

Then we must quietly and peaceably examine our Conscience, following therein the directions of our Ghostly Father. Which being done, we must endeavour to make an act of Contrition, which is so easy with God's grace, that a moment may conceive it, and an instant produce it;

it; and so powerful, that it obtains pardon of all we have offended in. Almighty God assures us of this by the mouth of his Prophet, saying, *Sigh, and you shall be saved.* But then it must proceed from love, and not from servile fear, as a good child, who grieves more for having displeased his Father, than for being disinherited by him.

Contrition consists not in tears or any sensible motion, for it may be had with a heart as cold as marble, and as hard as brass. But it consists in all spiritual operation of the will by which we detest sin, because it displeases and offends God, whom we are bound to love above all things. It must be universal, extending to all, without reserve of affection to any thing that is opposite to his Divine Love and liking. It must precede, if not Confession, at least Absolution.

A Prayer to beg Contrition.

Dear Jesus, I desire with my whole heart to have all the contrition for my sins that you desire I should have; but you know I cannot have it, unless you in your mercy bestow it upon me. It is what

what I most humbly beg by your Sacred Wounds and Precious Blood, *since you will not the Death of a Sinner, but rather that he be converted and live;* convert me then, and I shall be truly converted.

To move us to a true Contrition.

We may imagine ourselves at the feet of Christ Crucified, and that he says to us from the Cross, *What could I do more for you than I have done?* Let us look on the sad state he is reduced to for our sakes, and to satisfy for our sins, and to say to him,

Dear Lord, This is the work of your goodness and my malice, How can I behold it and not die with grief? How is it possible I can take content and pleasure, after having been the cause of all I see you suffer?

Dear Jesus, by the wounds I have caused you, and the Blood I have made you shed, and by your holy name which I have profaned, I beg you to have mercy on me, and to pardon me, for I heartily grieve for the very least of my offences, as having by them offended and dishonoured you. Yet I will hope in you, for

for however enormous my sins are, they cannot equal your mercies and merits; which merits I offer to your justice in full satisfaction for them.

Eternal Father, I offer you the infinite merits of your dear Son, in satisfaction for my sins, and to beg you will shew the efficacy of your Son's merits by granting me what I ask, which is pardon of sins, I ask it in his name, and your honour is engaged to hear him and them, whom he commands to ask in his name, and to whom he communicates his merits and credit. I am one of them, honour him therefore by granting me my request, since it is in his name I ask it.

Receive for me the satisfaction which Jesus your Son paid you on my account, dying on a Cross; that is abundantly sufficient to satisfy not only for my sins, but for those of all mankind; for the Sacred merits of my Saviour, pardon me all my offences.

I purpose, with the assistance of your grace, (which I hope to receive by means of this Sacrament) to fly from all that displeases you, and not to offend you deliberately in any thing; especially with your grace I will avoid such and such a sin, between this and my next Confession.

Let us not fail in this to secure the validity of our Confessions; which done, and being quite ready, let us say the following Prayer:

My God, I offer you the Confession I am going to make, for your greater glory, and to obey your will, and to render my soul more pleasing to you, by being washed in the Precious Blood of your Son, and to satisfy your Justice by humble Confession of my sins, and repair the dishonour they have done you, and to obtain your mercy and that Sanctifying Grace, which will preserve me from farther sins, and for all the intentions I ought to offer it for to gain whatever Pardon and Indulgence may be gained between this and next Confession, and that degree of your love and grace your mercy has designed me.

Since, dear Lord, you have shed your Blood for me, be pleased to apply the merits of it, by the absolution I am going to receive; one drop is sufficient to blot out,

out, and I confide in your goodness and mercy it will.

Grant to my soul, in making this Confession, all the requisite dispositions of Humility and perfect Contrition, which I ought to have in order to please and glorify you, and sanctify myself. Cast an eye of pity on my sinful soul, and regard not so much the evils I have done as your own infinite mercies, and the merits of my Saviour. If I have committed what deserves Damnation, he has done more than sufficient to merit my Salvation. With this confidence I will go to the Tribunal of your Mercies, in which I beg you will confirm in heaven the absolution I shall receive from your Minister on earth; and let it extend to all the sins of my life, all which I am truly sorry for, and abhor and detest them for love of you. I offer you the sorrow which your Divine Heart suffered at the sight of my sins, for that which is wanting in me. I beg, through the merits of that Sacred Heart, that you will cleanse me from them, and grant me the grace to avoid them for the future.

My Lord, I acknowledge that since my last Confession I have done much evil, and scarce any good; or if I have, it has been done with so much negligence, that it can be counted for nothing; in fine, the whole time since has been days void of virtue and full of irregularity. I am, dear Lord, an ungrateful, unfaithful, and perfidious Wretch, which deserves that you should shut for ever, in my regard, that wholesome Fountain which you have established in your Church, to wash me from my sins; this is what I might expect from your Justice; but when I reflect on your mercy, which is never wearied in seeking after the lost sheep; and when found, you treat it with an ineffable Sweetness; far from giving way to despair, I hope, with a firm confidence, the pardon of my offences, with which confidence I will go to the Tribunal of your Mercy to receive it.

When we go to Confession we must consider Christ as Chief and Supreme Priest, and, with joined hands and profound humility, make our Confession and desire rather to appear bad than good in the mind of our Confessor, for thereby God will receive greater glory, and we greater graces.

We

We must receive absolution as if Christ visibly gave it, since it is really he that gives it by the Mouth of the Priest, applying to our souls the Blood he shed upon Mount Calvary. Let us endeavour, in time of it, to increase our sorrow for all our sins, that we may concur with the Priest to the remission of them, and the infusion of God's Grace into our souls; for proportionably as we increase in sorrow, we shall receive augmentation of Grace.

Returning from Confession say,

My soul does magnify you, O Lord, and my spirit rejoices in you, my God and Saviour, because you have regarded the humility and penance of me your unworthy Creature; therefore, with your grace, the remainder of my life shall be blessed. Or else say, *Laudate Dominum omnes gentes,* &c.

Go straight to the choir, and, if possible, without speaking to any; and in thanksgiving to God for so great a benefit say,

Be pleased, dear Lord, to ratify in heaven the Absolution which your Minister has performed in your Name on earth;

receive the Confession I come from making, and finish the work your mercy has begun, by delivering me from these weaknesses and miseries my sins have caused in me; and grant me the grace never more deliberately to offend you.

Let my soul bless you, my God, and let all in me praise your most Holy Name, for having admitted me to this Sacrament. Let all your Saints and Angels praise you for it. Receive also those Praises and Thanks which your only Son, my God and Saviour, renders you, and will for ever pay you for the benefits which, through his merits, you are pleased to do us unworthy members.

I offer my Saviour's merits in satisfaction for all my defects in this or any other of my Confessions, begging pardon for them through the same merits, and that the Absolution which I have received from your Minister on earth, may extend to all the sins of my life, which I am heartily sorry for.

Receive, O Eternal Father, the satisfaction which my Saviour made you expiring on the Cross, and let it not only satisfy for all my debts to your Divine Majesty, but also obtain me the graces

necessary

necessary to amend what displeases you in me; and to love and serve you the remainder of my life as I ought.

Then with great Devotion and gratitude perform your Penance, and unite it with the merits of Christ; after which, it is advisable to accept, by way of Penance, of all the Crosses, Chagrins, and Mortifications which may befall us between this and our next Confession, as being ordained by Almighty God, who is pleased to add that Penance to that which has been given us in the Sacrament, both that we may satisfy for our sins, and increase our merit. Let us beg him to grant us the grace to make the best use of them.

Here we should renew the purpose, we made before Confession, of not voluntarily offending his Divine Majesty, especially by such or such a sin; but as we can do nothing of ourselves, we must not rely upon our resolutions, however strong they are, but upon God's assistant grace only, which he will not deny us if we ask it of him, through the merits of Christ, as we ought.

O Eternal Father, for the love you bear your Son, and for the glory he rendered

dered you by his death, pardon me all my sins, and give me the grace to avoid them for the future.

My God and Saviour, let the remembrance of this incomparable favour never go out of my memory; let me think thereof day and night, and never without gratitude and love; and grant me the grace that the author of all good be ever present to my mind. It is he who, by a mercy that cannot be sufficiently admired, pardons me all my sins, when the pardon of one only is a favour that a thousand years services cannot worthily acknowledge: How then can I acknowledge a goodness that remits me innumerable ones?

The remainder of the day we must, with the Divine Assistance, be careful to comport ourselves so as to do nothing unworthy of the grace conferred on us in the Sacrament of Penance.

From which time we ought to begin to prepare ourselves for Communion, by a great desire to receive Christ, in whose Precious Blood our souls have been washed. We may say from time to time,

Sweet Jesus, since your love is not content with what you have already done for me, me, by applying your Precious Blood to my soul, to wash it from its Offences; but you also invite me to receive yet a greater favour, to wit, your Divine Self. Dispose my heart, I beseech you, for it, for none but you can do it.

A Prayer to our Blessed Lady, to beg the due Dispositions for Communion.

O most Blessed Virgin, and most worthy Mother of God, whom you conceived in your chaste Womb, whose adorable Body and Blood he received from you. It concerns you that he be received with all the respect and honour he deserves, and that he be not unworthily treated by those on whom he bestows himself with so much love. It is therefore that I address myself to you, to beg you will obtain of him for me all the blessings I stand in need of, to receive him worthily. Beg him to take possession of my heart by love, before he enters my body by the Sacrament. Obtain of him for me, all the Dispositions and Virtues which may render me pleasing to him, especially those two, which rendered you deservedly his Mother, which is
Purity

Purity and Humility, that he may find nothing in me that may favour of either impurity or pride, both which I detest from my heart, and am resolved, for the future, to endeavour to acquire the two contrary Virtues, thereby to please him and imitate you; begging for this, his grace, by your all-powerful intercession, which I now implore with my whole heart.

CHAPTER VIII.

Of Communion.

SEC. I.

Three Days Preparation for Communion, before all great Feasts.

The Blessed Sacrament which we are to receive, is the pledge of eternal life, and our Viaticum to bring us to it. It must put us in mind of the end for which God created us, and placed us in this world; which was, to render us happy to Eternity, of the same happiness which his Divine Majesty and his Saints enjoy. To prepare ourselves for this Divine Sacrament,

crament, besides the ordinary preparation, which consists in a greater care to perform our Spiritual actions well, and to avoid all offence of God, a withdrawing from all unnecessary discourses; more frequent aspirations to beg of his Divine Majesty, whatever may dispose us for Confession and Communion; and the practice of Mortification and Self-denial, especially as to what may be necessay for the performing all our duties well: Besides all this, I say, we should do well to observe that which follows:

For the first Day.

1. Address yourself to the Eternal Father, who, out of his pure goodness, has made choice of you, to make you happy for Eternity with his own happiness, and nourishes you with his own food, which is the knowledge, love, and enjoyment of himself.

2. Admire his goodness, thank him for it, and beg his Divine Majesty to grant you the grace worthily to prepare yourself for Communion, which is a foretaste of that happiness.

3. Address

3. Address yourself to our Blessed Lady, as to her that was first chosen for that happiness, begging her, in your behalf, to return the Eternal Father thanks for creating you for that end; and beseech her to obtain you the grace to communicate worthily, saying three *Ave Marias* for that effect.

If it be the feast of some Saint, congratulate with him for his Felicity, and beg him to pray for you, that you may worthily receive that God he beholds face to face.

Second Day.

1. Address yourself to God the Son, by whose merits you have been chosen for Eternal Bliss, and who, by his Cross and Blood, has marked the place for each of his Elect.

Consider how much he laboured and suffered to open the gates of heaven for you, and to merit you the grace to arrive to that bliss; among other means he has left himself in the most Blessed Sacrament, that by receiving him who is the Holy of Holies, you may become holy here and happy for Eternity.

2. Thank

2. Thank our Saviour for all he has done and suffered, to open heaven to you, and to make you a Saint. Beg him by the merit of his Communion on the eve of his Death, when he received himself in that Divine Sacrament, that you may worthily receive him, and so render the labours and pains he has taken for you, fruitful and efficacious.

3. Beg our Blessed Lady, who conceived him, and afterwards, by frequent Communions, received him, and thereby so great a degree of Sanctity, that she would please to obtain you the dispositions you ought to have to receive him worthily, for which effect say three *Ave Marias*.

4. If it be the feast of some Saint, congratulate with the Saint, for having made such good use of the Precious Blood and merits of Christ, as to possess the glory he merited for him. Beg the Blessed Saint to obtain you the grace so to communicate, that it may merit you the possession of the glory your Saviour has purchased for you.

The Third Day.

1. Address yourself to the Holy Ghost, by whose Grace and Aid you must acquire the Sanctity which Christ has purchased for you. Admire the diverse means he makes use of to draw your affections from the things of this World, and to bring you to true Sanctity.

2. Thank him for all the inspirations and lights he has given you, in order to your attaining true Sanctity, which is found in real Purity of Heart. Beg the Divine Spirit to purify and dispose yours to receive him.

3. Beg our Blessed Lady, as she is Spouse to the Holy Ghost, to obtain for you of that Divine Spirit, the like dispositions which she had in her soul whenever she communicated; for that effect say three *Ave Marias*.

4. If the Feast be of any Saint, congratulate with the Saint for having so well followed the motions of the Holy Ghost, as thereby to have gained so great Sanctity. Beg him to obtain you the grace, so to confess and communicate, that you may

may attain to that degree of Sanctity which God requires of you.

SEC. II.

Three Days Preparation for Communion,

Before the Feasts of our Blessed Lady.

Besides the ordinary Preparations, as page 154 and 155, we should do well to make the following reflections.

For the Morning of the First Day.

1. Reflect, and give thanks to God the Father for chusing the Blessed Virgin for his Daughter, and for all the favours and graces he did her on that account.

2. Thank his Divine Majesty for that, through his mercy, he has chosen you for his adopted child, and for giving you all helps to render you worthy of that honour. Offer him in return all the thanks that are rendered him in heaven and upon earth.

3. Beg him, by the merits of our Blessed Lady, to grant you the grace to make so good a Confession and Communion,

that you may thereby obtain the eternal inheritance he has designed you as his child.

In the Afternoon.

1. Rejoice, and congratulate with our Blessed Lady, for being chosen, particularly before all others, to be Daughter to the Eternal Father. Reflect on the Privileges and Advantages she has by the same.

2. Beg our Lady to obtain for you the grace to confess and communicate, after such a manner, that you may by means of the same be for ever numbered amongst the children and Elect of God.

For the Morning of the second Day.

1. Reflect, and give thanks to God the Son for having chosen our Blessed Lady before all others, for his most Blessed Mother, and for giving her all that was suitable to so high a dignity.

2. Thank our Saviour for mercifully designing you a like favour by Holy Communion; since you are to receive into your Breast, the same Jesus she bore in her Womb.

3. Beg

3. Beg him, for the merits of his Blessed Mother, to grant you a share of those graces and favours he bestowed upon her, that you may worthily bear in your bosom him she carried in her Womb.

For the Afternoon.

1. Rejoice, and congratulate with our Blessed Lady, for the choice her Son made of her to be his Mother, and for giving her the grace to merit that title by her actions.

2. Beg her to obtain you the grace worthily to receive her Son; and that you may, by this Communion, supply for the defects you have committed in your others.

For the Morning of the third Day.

1. Reflect, and give thanks to God the Holy Ghost, for having chosen the Blessed Virgin, before all others, to be his Sacred Spouse, and for having adorned her soul as was requisite for such a dignity.

2. Thank the Divine Spirit for having espoused you to himself in Holy Baptism and

and Holy Religion, and for being pleased to visit and dwell in your soul, by Holy Communion, as in his Temple.

3. Beg him so to adorn your soul, as to render it a worthy and pleasing habitation to his Divine Majesty.

For the Afternoon.

1. Rejoice, and congratulate with our Blessed Lady for that infinite honour of being Spouse to God the Holy Ghost, and for the merits he gave her to render her worthy of it.

2. Beg her to obtain you requisite graces to perform well so important an action as is Communion.

SEC. III.

On Ordinary Communion Eves.

Besides the ordinary preparation, 154 and 155, we must entertain our thoughts as follows.

For

For the Morning.

1. Reflect on the great Desire our Lord had to institute and receive with his Apostles, this Holy Sacrament, *With a longing desire* (says he) *have I desired to eat this Pasche with you before I suffer.*

2. To excite a great desire to receive him who pleased so ardently to desire the giving himself to us. Let us reflect who it is that comes; the end for which he comes; and the advantages which we shall receive by his coming, if we on our side prepare ourselves well to receive him.

3. Beg our Blessed Lady, by the ardent desire she had to receive her Divine Son in this adorable Sacrament, to obtain you a great desire of that happiness.

After Dinner.

1. Reflect upon the Humility which our Lord practised before he instituted this Sacrament, washing the feet of his Apostles; and then remaining alone without splendor, or lustre in this adorable Mystery, to shew us how pleasing this virtue

virtue is to him, and how necessary to dispose us for Communion.

2. During the day make acts of it, acknowledging yourself not only nothing, but worse than nothing, by reason of your sins; and if any honour be rendered you, receive it not as due to you, but refer it all to God.

3. Beg our Lady, by her great humility, which drew the Almighty into her Womb, and rendered her so pleasing to him, to obtain you that virtue, and say the *Salve Regina* for that effect.

After Vespers.

1. Reflect that our Lord, by washing his Apostles' feet before he gave himself to them, would give us to understand the Purity with which we ought to approach to Holy Communion.

2. That you may obtain this Purity, you must, by frequent acts of Contrition, endeavour to expiate your past sins, and be careful not to commit new ones.

3. Beg our Blessed Lady, by the great Purity with which she received God into her Womb, and afterwards into her breast by Holy Communion, to obtain
you

you what is necessary and fitting to communicate worthily.

SEC. IV.

For Communion.

After having performed all that belongs to Confession, we should wholly entertain our thoughts with what may dispose us for Communion; and as Spiritual Communion is the best Disposition for the Sacramental, so we cannot do better than to communicate Spiritually from time to time. This is done by believing God present, and humbling ourselves to our own nothing, ardently desiring (if so happy as to be in the State of Grace) to receive him for the same end for which he would be received; which is, that he may live in us and we in him.

Jesus comes to each soul in Communion, to unite himself to her after a particular manner, according to the degree of perfection he calls her to, every one having a particular degree which distinguishes her from another, and the graces given in Communion are to advance her to that degree which God has designed her.

To concur with God's designs, and prepare and dispose ourselves to receive those graces he intends us by Communion, let us from six o'clock over night (if not hindered by obedience or charity) withdraw ourselves from all other concerns, and entirely give our attention to what may dispose and prepare us for Communion; being careful to keep the silence ordained by our statutes for that effect.

In order to animate us the more to this practice, and to incline us to employ that hour in some pious duties; we may reflect that it was at the same hour, to wit, six o'clock, that Christ on the Eve of his Passion eat the Paschal Lamb with his Apostles, and instituted this Sacrament, which he did as his own words express it.

1. That he might remain with us for ever.
2. That it might be to us a perpetual memory of his Death and Passion, suffered for our sakes.
3. That as he lived for his Father, so we might live for him, by receiving him in the Blessed Sacrament.

As these were our Lord's designs in instituting this Sacrament, so they must be ours in receiving him; and we must not only beg him to effect them in us, but must also on our side concur to the same.

We should do well to reflect and see over night, what intentions we design to communicate for, and to offer our Communion then, repeating the same again the next morning before we communicate, a proper time for which is the offertory of the Mass; and it may be done as follows.

General Intentions for Communion.

Since you are pleased, my God, to express so great a desire that I receive you, as to threaten me with punishment if I refuse to come, (though no punishment, dear Lord, could equal that of being deprived of this happiness!) 'tis to obey your Blessed Will that I approach, and I offer this Communion in obedience to your divine Will; for the increase of your glory; for all the designs you had in instituting this adorable Sacrament, and for those you have over my soul; to beg

they

they may be perfectly accomplished, and that you may be in me what you should be, and may destroy in me what is mine, and opposite to you, taking an entire possession of my heart, that I may be united to you with a more perfect love.

'Tis to obtain the accomplishment of your promises, to wit, *That those who eat your Flesh, and drink your Blood, shall live for ever.* And *as you live for your Father, so those that receive you, shall live for you.* 'Tis likewise to obtain the pardon of my sins and offences; grace to overcome all my spiritual enemies, and to be faithful to your love in all temptations; also to beg an increase of charity and all other virtues, especially a perfect submission to your blessed will in all the accidents of this life.

Grant that the receiving your Sacred Body, which I do in memory of, and thanksgiving for your most bitter Death and Passion suffered for me, may be to me a pledge of Eternal Life. I offer it also for the exaltation of our Holy Mother the Church, for the extirpation of Heresies, and conversion of all Misbelievers; for Peace and Union among Christian Kings and Princes; and for all

the

the intentions for which I ought to offer it: also to get whatever pardon or indulgence may be gained; and moreover for all the intentions which may be for the increase of your Honour and Glory: and to beg you will please to augment your grace in the hearts of all your Elect, especially those I am obliged to pray for, as N. N. and each one of this Community, which I beseech you to bless, preserve, and keep united in the bond of perfect Charity.

Besides these general intentions, 'tis advisable to join some particular ones, according to the view or design proposed to ourselves in each Communion; as to partake of the Mystery of the Feast we solemnize; to correct some fault; to acquire some particular virtue which we find the greatest want of; to return thanks for some grace or favour which we have received; to obtain the spirit of our particular examen, and the grace to be faithful in it; to pray for any that have recommended themselves to our Prayers, &c.

We must endeavour at night immediately before we go to rest, and in the morning as soon as awake, to possess our minds

minds with the happiness we hope for, which is to receive God, begging him to give us due dispositions to receive him worthily.

Aspirations at our First Awaking.

O my God, I offer my heart and soul, in which this day you design to lodge; take them, for they are yours, and prepare them as you would have them prepared.

The duties we are employed in from that time till Holy Mass, are the fittest to dispose us for Communion, they being the Divine Office and mental Prayer: let us endeavour to perform them in such a manner that we may be thereby duly disposed.

As Holy Communion is an action of the greatest importance, and that we cannot of ourselves have due dispositions unless God is pleased to give them to us; therefore to obtain them of him we cannot do better than to address ourselves to our Blessed Lady, she having the most interest in the worthy reception of her Son, and also the most power to obtain us all that is necessary for that

that effect; and as she is our Mother, she is truly desirous of our good; and what greater good can she procure us than to receive the Body and Blood of her Son in such a manner that we may partake of his spirit, and be united to him for time and for Eternity.

Another motive for making our addresses to her, is to render ourselves more pleasing to our dear Redeemer who chose to come to us by her means, so we cannot do better than by her means and under her Protection, to go to him; nor can we offer him any thing more acceptable, or of greater value (next to his own merits) than those of his Blessed Mother, to supply for what is wanting in us.

At the Beginning of the Mass.

Offer to Christ the enflamed Love, and Holy Dispositions with which his Blessed Mother presented both him and herself to his Eternal Father in the Temple; to supply for what is wanting in you, and beg our Lady to make you partaker of it by her intercession, that you may the more worthily receive her Divine Son.

At the Kyries. Offer to our Saviour his Blessed Mother's Hatred and entire separation from the least sin or offence, and for her merits, beg him to pardon all those you have committed.

At the Gospel. Offer him her Faith, which was the source of all her happiness, and made her prefer God's Will to all other advantages; so present her perfect Faith to obtain Pardon for your having so often done the contrary.

At the Offertory. Take up your thoughts, and unite yourself to that perfect Adoration which Christ renders to his Eternal Father; and congratulate with our Lady that her Son only can worthily honour God: beg her to obtain you the grace to adore him in spirit and truth, and to be ever grateful to him for his mercies to you, and to be willing to satisfy his Justice, by patiently suffering whatever he shall permit.

From Sanctus till the Elevation. To obey Christ's Orders in commemorating his Death and Passion, accompany our Lady in spirit, and remain with her at the foot of the Cross, where she stood immoveable.

immoveable. There it was that her soul was pierced with the sword of grief at the sight of her suffering Son, yet ever perfectly submissive to the will of God. Who can express what she suffered when she heard her Divine Son complain of being abandoned by his Eternal Father! with respect she adored the Divine Conduct, at the same time so holy and afflicting! she could not sweeten the bitterness of her Son's Chalice, but she honoured the Sovereign Authority of his Father which made him suffer so.

Here we must humble ourselves and beg pardon, acknowledging we are the unhappy cause of the sufferings, both of the Son and of the Mother; begging our Lady to obtain that the merit of those sufferings may be now applied to our souls to make them fitter habitations for her Divine Son.

At the Pater Noster. We ought to say it with the Priest, and unite ourselves both to the sentiments of Christ when he taught it, and to our Lady's when she recited it.

At Agnus Dei. Reflect that this Divine Lamb without spot, which our Lady bore nine months in her womb, and which was slain for our salvation, will enter our hearts to apply the Precious Blood he shed, thereby to purify them from the spots and stains of sin; let us beg our Lady to obtain us due dispositions to receive the full benefit of that Precious Blood.

The happy moment drawing near which will put us in possession of our God, we must with a new fervour dispose ourselves by the following Acts.

Of Faith.

I firmly believe that in this Sacrament is contained my God and Saviour, who gave his life for my Salvation, and through whose merits I only hope it. I believe 'tis the same Lord who while he remained on earth raised the dead and cured the sick, and never refused to succour those that addressed themselves to him, and that he is not less powerful and willing now, than he was then.

Of Hope.

Dear Lord, what may I not expect and hope from your love, who in your
Death

Death gave yourself for me, and in this Sacrament still give yourself to me? I hope for no less than the accomplishment of the promises you are pleased to make to them that shall receive you in this Sacrament; and that you will apply to my soul the merits of your Passion, and give me those graces which are the fruit of your Death; and that you will not permit that my receiving this Sacrament, which you instituted for my Salvation, and which I do to obey your will, should through any unworthiness of mine prove my condemnation.

Of Love.

Give yourself to me, my God, for I love you, but if not enough, make me love you more. I am going to cast myself into your arms, nay into your heart, let me never be separated from you; take possession of mine, which truly desires to receive you, that so I may be for ever united to you.

Of Humility.

What am I, O my God, that you should come to me! I acknowledge myself infinitely unworthy of this honour; for though I had the burning flames of the Seraphims, and your Blessed Mother's fullness of grace, I should be still infinitely unworthy to receive you. What then must I be who am so far from this, that I have no good in me! and therefore I own myself unworthy of the least of your favours, and much more of this; but since it is your will that I receive you, purify my heart before you enter it; say but the word, and my soul shall be saved.

Of Desire.

Come, sweet Jesus, for I truly desire to receive you. Give yourself to me, and that suffices me; but in giving yourself to me, grant me the grace to give myself entirely to you: for Communion does not only give you to me, but also gives me to you, according to your own words, *he that eats my Flesh remains in me, and I in him*; and again, *he that eats me, me, the same shall live by me.* Grant me but that, and I desire no more.

Of Obedience.

Lord, since 'tis your will and pleasure that I should receive you, commanding me to come, if I would have my part with you, I approach, yet no ways presuming on myself, but relying on your goodness, which I know to be infinite, hoping you will receive in mercy her, who comes to you with confidence, and acknowledges no good in herself, but much the contrary. If your Divine Eye sees any sin in my soul which might render it criminal, I beg you will forgive it, for with my whole heart I detest it, and all that may offend or displease you in me.

Offering.

Dear Lord, in lieu of those dispositions which are wanting in me, I offer you all the Love, Humility, Purity, Devotion, and other Preparations with which you have been received by all pious souls, and even by your Blessed Mother, wishing

wishing they were all mine for no other end than that I might receive you more worthily.

Petition.

O my God, grant me those dispositions which I ought to have, and which you only can give me, that I may not only receive your precious Body and Blood, but the effects and virtue of them; so that in receiving you I may partake of your spirit, and be united to you for time and for eternity, which I ardently desire.

Dear Lord, receive yourself in the midst of my heart, and glorify yourself there, as it shall be most agreeable to you: and let your love and divine dispositions supply for all that is wanting in me. And as there is no place worthy of you but yourself, nor any love with which you can be worthily received, but that which you have for yourself, that you may be worthily received in me, I annihilate myself at your feet and all that is in me, and give myself to you, that coming to me by Communion, you may be received not in me, but in yourself, and with the love

love you bear yourself; and (that way) as worthily as you deserve.

With this disposition, of being nothing in your own conceit, and desire nothing but the possession of God, approach to Holy Communion, for it is of all others the best.

Enter, dear Lord, into your own, which is my heart and soul: come and dwell for ever there. Let it never be said that you come into your own, and your own would not receive you. I desire nothing more than to possess you, and never be separated from you.

SEC. VI.

The Necessity and Advantages of employing well the Time after Communion.

It is not only the want of a due preparation before Communion which renders our Communion fruitless, but also the not employing well the time after; the not managing those precious and favourable moments as we ought, in which our Lord remains with us. In each of those moments he both can and would bestow great favours upon us, if we did but dispose ourselves to receive them, or

at

at least did not put an obstacle to them, by any voluntary distraction or dissipation of mind; had it not been for this, the graces we should have received in Holy Communion would have worked wonders in us, for we might gain in one Communion sufficient to enrich us for ever.

How we ought to employ those precious Moments.

1. To adore, with profound respect, the most God's Divinity really presents in our breast.

2. To adore the Sacred Humanity, and those wounds he received in it for us, thanking him for them and for all he suffered, begging he will be pleased to apply the merits of them to our souls.

3. To offer him and his merits to his Eternal Father, for to acknowledge his infinite being, to thank him for all his benefits, to satisfy for our sins, and to obtain all we stand in need of for our Eternal Salvation.

4. To offer ourselves, and all we have, in thanksgiving; and not content with that, to offer the praises of Angels and men.

5. To

5. To recommend those we have any obligation to pray for, or those who have recommended themselves to our Prayers, as also to petition for the souls in Purgatory.

6. To beg pardon for all defects committed in this or any other Communion.

7. To offer as a grateful return, the amendment of some fault, or the practice of some virtue between this and the next Communion.

8. Lastly, To beg our Saviour to bestow his blessing on us, and on our endeavours.

A Manner of performing the same.

My Lord and my God, I adore you present in me with all the respect I am capable of. I acknowledge you as Author of my Being, and my final End. I render you thanks, with all the extent of my heart, for this inestimable favour; your power, though infinite, cannot bestow a greater.

I offer, in return, all the adorations and praises of the Blessed above; all those which the Sacred Humanity of Christ rendered you; and those of his most Blessed

sed Mother, after he took Flesh in her Sacred Womb.

My sweet Saviour and dear Redeemer, I adore your Sacred Humanity, and your soul full of love for me, as also those Sacred Wounds which you received in your Body for my Salvation. I render you infinite thanks for them, and for all you suffered, and humbly beg you will now apply the merits of them to my soul.

My dear Saviour, you are in me living and operating towards your Eternal Father, rendering him those homages which are due to him, and this you desire to do in the hearts of all your Elect, even to the end of the World. O do it now in mine, and permit me to render them with you: I unite my heart with yours for that purpose, and with you, and by you I desire to adore, praise, and love him.

O Eternal Father, who, out of your infinite Mercy and Love, have given me your only Son, with all the treasures of his merits, to dispose and offer as my own for your glory, and my own particular profit, being pleased for that end to have me receive him into my breast, as mine and united with me.

In

In union then of that Charity, wherewith you give him to me, and that wherewith he offered himself for me upon the Cross, and now gives himself to me in this Adorable Sacrament: I offer him and his infinite merits for the everlasting Praise and Glory of your Name, and in acknowledgment of your Sovereignty and Divine Being. I offer him, and all the Praises and Thanks he rendered you while on earth, in acknowledgment of all the favours and benefits you have bestowed on his Sacred Humanity, on his most Blessed Mother, on the whole Church, and on my unworthy self.

I offer him, and all his Pains, Labours, and Sufferings, in satisfaction for all the sins that have ever been committed, my own in particular.

I offer him and his merits to supply for all that is wanting in me, and to obtain of your mercies all that is necessary to render me agreeable to your Divine Majesty, and to secure my Salvation. It is in his merits I put all my trust.

As this Offering is infinitely pleasing to your Sovereign Majesty, I extend my requests for the whole Church, begging you will replenish the soul of our Holy Father

Father the Pope, and all Prelates and Christian Princes, with all the Graces necessary to acquit themselves worthily of their charges. For sinners, I beg the sentiments of true Contrition, and the grace to change and amend their lives. For those in the state of Grace, that they may increase in all virtues. For Infidels and Misbelievers, that they may be converted to the true Faith.

I most humbly recommend to your mercies all those I am obliged to pray for, as, each one of this Family, and all my Friends and Relations, beseeching you, for the sake of your dear Son, whom I have now received, to give them your grace in such abundance that they may perfectly love and serve you. I beg the same for my Enemies, whom I pardon with all my heart, and beg yours for them.

Lastly, I beg you to solace and deliver the poor suffering souls in Purgatory, for the merits of our Saviour's precious Blood shed for them, especially N. N. Let your mercy which has pardoned them the impieties of their sins, put an end to their punishment, that they may be speedily

speedily translated to the state of glory for which you eternally designed them.

Then turning to our dear Saviour say, Dear Jesus, you give yourself to me with an infinite love, with the same I desire to return myself to you, which I do in all the manners I am able, by the promises of my Baptism, and by the vows of my profession, all which I here renew, and beg your grace to observe them constantly: I give myself to you to dispose of as you please, desiring, as far as in me lies, to give you a more special power over my Body, Soul, Heart, and Actions, leaving myself and all that belongs to me to your loving Providence, and to the disposition of your will, with the care and success of all my affairs, begging you will please to give me the grace in all I do, to have for end the advancement of your glory, and the accomplishment of your Blessed Will.

I confide, my sweet Saviour, in your goodness, that having given yourself to me, you will not deny me what I want for your glory and my good. I cannot, dear Lord, doubt of your Love, after all you have done for me; but since my God you love me, how can you see my afflictions

tions and not comfort me? Can you see me have so little love for you, and not enflame my heart with more? though you should refuse me all things else, yet grant me that.

Your Heart, my dear Saviour, is full of Love for me; it is that which brings you to so vile a Creature as I am. O in-created Love! what is it you require of me! nothing but that I love you, and be wholly yours; which I can never be so long as I remain tied to the love of myself, to my own Judgment and conceits, to every little will of mine, and to my reputation; whereas you require self-hatred for your love, and that forgetting all things else I should seek nothing but you. O my God, it is your all-powerful hand that can effect this in me, let it be done to me according to your will, and the amorous designs of your heart. Take, dear Lord, possession of my heart, which has the Honour to possess you; and love, and glorify yourself in me in all the manners you would be loved and glorified, and suffer nothing in me to rebel against your Will.

Here lay upon all your miseries to him, and urge for a remedy, since it is his will

will you should. Ask whatever grace or favour you have need of, with great confidence; and if you know not what to ask in particular, desire our Lord, who knows your necessities, and the designs for which he gives himself to you in this Sacrament, and the effects which, by means of it, he works in souls, that he will accordingly give you, and work in you what shall be most pleasing to him. Say to his Divine Majesty,

To whom can a child better address herself than to her Father; you are mine, dear Lord, I acknowledge no other: O shew yourself a Father, and permit me no longer to continue in my imperfections, especially those that oppose your designs. Give me a pure heart and perseverance in your service; grant that I may frequently lift up my thoughts to you, and ever walk in your presence by Faith, Hope, Charity, and Conformity to your Will. Take from me all those dispositions which are contrary to your Spirit, and give me the bowels of Charity, that I may always compassionate the Weak, Sick, and Afflicted, support the Imperfect, encourage and help the Perfect, and make myself all to gain them all to it all to you: Sanctify me, that I may contribute to the Sanctification of others.

Let your patience be ever present to me in all adversities; your obedience in my submission to the orders of your Providence; and your Charity in supporting my neighbours, and labouring for their Salvation. Give me great confidence in your paternal Providence, and the grace to remain firm in your love during my whole life.

After the happiness of possessing you, I have but one thing more to wish, which is, that I may see and for ever enjoy you, whom I have had the happiness to receive: and I have all reason to hope it, for you not only give me your word for it, but you also give me yourself as pledge of it; saying, *He that eats this Bread of Life, shall live for ever.* I firmly hope it, and this though I should have committed all the sins of the world, yet I would not despair of mercy and pardon as soon as I asked it with an humble and contrite heart.

Then kiss the Sacred Wounds of Jesus, by them begging pardon for your sins; and at his feet beg true humility and the knowledge of yourself; at his right hand, purity

purity of intention; at his left, patience in sufferings; at his side, the love of God and your neighbour; all which beg thro' those affections he felt in his heart when he received the Wounds in his Body.

O sweet and unspotted soul of Jesus, since you are a voluntary prisoner, I cannot nor must not let you go till you bless me; vouchsafe, dear Lord, your Benediction both on me and all my actions, that they may succeed to your greater glory: and as you used to do when on earth, leave in my soul the marks of your sweet presence, to supply for your absence.

I recommend to your mercy all those I am obliged to pray for, as, each one of this Community, my Friends, Relations, and Benefactors, especially all those who have helped me towards you; give them your Divine Spirit, and all the graces necessary to be truly pleasing to you; accomplish in them, and in me, all the merciful designs your providence has had over us from all Eternity.

Pardon, dear Lord, the unworthiness, indevotion, and all other defects with which I have now or ever received you, and permit them not to deprive me of the
fruit

fruit which otherways your Sacred Body would communicate to me.

O most Sacred Lady, Mother of my Saviour, I return you humble thanks for the happiness I have possessed, and I beseech you to thank your dear Son for me, and to supply for my defects, offer him all the services you rendered him when on earth: and for his sake, who gave me to you in the Person of Saint John, own me for your Child, and shew yourself a Mother to me, whom next to your Son I love, and place my trust in.

Then, in return of thanks for the honour received, offer whatever you think his Divine Majesty requires of you, or what may render you more pleasing to him; as for example, a greater Fidelity in your particular Examen. If you are much given to seek your own ease, resolve to mortify yourself in that point. If you seek yourself even in spiritual things more than God's glory, beg his grace that for the future you may sacrifice all things to that end. If you judge others, or speak of their defects, resolve between this and your next Communion to fall no more into that fault. This will be the most acceptable return we can make

make our dear Lord for his kind visit; and by so doing we shall reap due profit from the Sacraments.

SEC. VII.

Another Manner of Entertainment after Communion.

Which consists in a great calm and recollection, where the soul, humbled in the presence of God, in her tastes how sweet he is.

O happy hour (may she say) which blesses me with the presence of you my God and Saviour! my heart is more content with possessing you than if it had the whole World! I desire but one thing more, which is, to be never separated from you who are the soul of my soul, and heart of my heart!

The principal occupation of those happy moments in which Christ remains in us (that is, as long as the Sacramental species remain) is to abandon ourselves entirely to his love, and sweetly to enjoy his presence. If we speak, they should be only words which love suggests, as these, pausing upon each: *I have found whom*

*whom my soul loves——nothing shall separate me from him——My God and my All——My beloved is mine, and I will be all his——*Each furnishes sufficient matter for thought and affection: and as long as we find that, we rest in it.

Then we may keep ourselves with great humility at our dear Saviour's feet, adoring him with astonishment that that infinite Majesty, before whom Seraphims tremble and all Nature is but a point, should come to visit us! then passing to acts of thanksgiving; and being sensible of our incapacity of performing it as we ought, we must invite all creatures to do it for us, and offer him all the love of the Blessed in Heaven, and of all his faithful Servants upon earth who receive him. Finally, we must offer him his own earth, with all the immensity it contains.

Then again rest sweetly at his feet, seeking after no more, because we possess our All in him, who is our God; sensible that we love him not as he deserves, but well pleased that he is so amiable that none can duly love him. Say to him, dear Lord, I owe you more than I can repay you, but not more than

than I would render you, were it in my power; though I am far from desiring to be quit of my obligations to you.

Then consider him as the life of your soul; beg him to sanctify it, that it may be a more fit habitation for him; also beseech him to quicken your spirit, and enflame your heart: then enter by consideration into his, and see how ardently that Divine Heart loved his Eternal Father from his incarnation till his expiring on the Cross. He sought nothing but to do his will, increase his glory, and pay him homage; which he still desires to do in the hearts of his Elect to the end of the world; beg him to do it in you, and sweetly unite yourself to all he shall do in you.

See then what that Sacred Heart of our dear Saviour may dislike in you, and purpose the amendment of it. Consider what his designs are over you, and what he requires of you; reflect what most hinders you from doing it, and resolve to do better for the future, begging his grace for that effect, without which we can do nothing.

Having performed this, you may retire, but let it be in recollection, which we should endeavour to maintain during the whole day: This is necessary to draw profit from Holy Communion; for if our Lord's Divine Spirit remains no longer with us than his Body, (which is but while the Sacramental Species remain) our souls will not draw due nourishment from so divine a food. Since our Divine Visitor opens his heart to us, and is willing to have us retire there, let us then take up our lodging and remain there; so keeping ourselves from the reach of all that might disquiet us.

To maintain in us the spirit of gratitude for so special a favour, (nothing being so displeasing to God as ingratitude) we may, from time to time, make use of those following aspirations.

Let all in me praise you, Lord, for coming in person to visit me.

Put yourself as a seal upon my soul, that nothing may enter it which displeases you.

Sanctify the place of your footsteps, which this day has been my heart.

What shall I render you for all you have done for me?

My soul, bless our Lord for all his mercies to you.

SEC.

SEC. VIII.

When Tempted.

To feed on God, and not to live according to the laws of his love, is horrible!

Shall I offend God, who this day has honoured me with his presence?

When we practise some Act of Virtue,

We should offer it in return of thanks for the great favour we received in the morning.

As when we are called to the Divine Office, make of it a Sacrifice of thanksgiving.

When we sit at Table,

Let us think of the happiness we have had this day, to be invited to the Table of Angels, and to feed on God himself.

By this means we shall not only return thanks, but also dispose ourselves for the next Communion; for a Religious Life is the best disposition for Communion, and

Communion is a new engagement to a Religious Life. By this means Jesus will live in us, and we shall live for him, which is one of the admirable Effects of this Sacrament, it making us live for him who died for us.

We should be miserable if we partook only of the Body of Christ, and not of his Spirit: If we receive the one, and reject the other, we frustrate God's designs. Now to partake of his Spirit, we must enter into his Sentiments, and love and practise what he loved and practised, avoiding and hating what he hates.

The chief fruit we are to draw from Holy Communion, is to become one with Jesus in Spirit; this being his petition to his Father: That as his Father and he were one, we should be one with him in spirit. This we can never arrive to by our own strength; Jesus, whom we receive, will give it us if we ask it, and on our parts concur with his Grace. One Communion is sufficient to make us Saints.

It may be a help to devotion and attention, to receive Christ after different notions; for Example, as our Father, our Pastor, our Physician, our Soul's
Guest,

Guest, our Viaticum: Sometimes in one manner, and sometimes in another, as may suit best with our present disposition; foreseeing over-night after what manner we design to receive him, that at our awaking in the morning we may enter into the disposition of it, which you will find at the end of the Book.

FOR HOLY COMMUNION.

A Second Manner of preparing for Communion.

Intentions for Communion.

My God, I offer my Communion in obedience to your Will, and for your greater Honour and Glory, and in thanksgiving to you, for having instituted this Divine Sacrament, and requiring that I, though so unworthy, should receive you, which I do to obey your Will, and for the accomplishment of all your merciful designs, in entering my heart by this Divine Sacrament, desiring to receive and possess you, but for the end for which you would be received.

I offer it also in memory and thanksgiving for your bitter Death and Passion; and to beg that the fruit of it may be applied to my soul, and that I may be united to you in as perfect a manner as you require, and that you may live in me, and I of your Spirit, and that you would enlighten my understanding and moderate my Passions, and grant me the Victory over them and all that displeases you, and pardon me my sins, and give me the grace to be faithful to your Love in all temptations, and a perfect submission to your Will in all occasions.

I also offer it in honour of your Divine Providence, and in thanksgiving for its effects, and merciful designs in my regard, and to obtain the grace to abandon myself to its decrees, and to confide in it in all events.

For each Sunday of the Month as follows.

First Sunday. In honour of the Blessed Trinity and Thanksgiving for my Baptism, and to beg that I may perfectly fulfil the promises made for me thereat, and the gift of Faith, Hope, and Charity.

Second

Second Sunday. In honour of our Saviour's humanity, and all the mysteries of his life, especially his Nativity and Infancy, and to beg humility and simplicity of heart.

Third Sunday. In honour of the years of his private Life, labouring and working with his Mother and St. Joseph for our Example, and to beg his Blessing on all my works, and that he will unite them to his, give me a pure intention in seeking but to please him by doing his Will.

Fourth Sunday. In honour and thanksgiving for our Saviour's Death and Passion, and to beg Salvation of my soul and pardon of my sins, and the Spirit of Penance, and the Grace to draw that profit from the consideration of his Passion, as he would have me, and the grace of a happy death. I offer it in honour of your most Holy Mother, and in thanksgiving for the Election of her, and for having created her so perfect both for his Glory and Good of all mankind, and for giving her to me for Mother; begging you will, for her sake, give me all the qualities of a worthy child and servant of her's.

I offer it also in thanksgiving, for giving one of your Heavenly Princes for my Guardian, and for all the Gifts of Grace and Glory you bestowed on him; begging I may always comport myself towards him as you require I should.

I offer it in honour of all your Saints, and to thank you for the Gifts and Graces you bestowed on them in this life, and for the Glory you have rendered them in the other, especially those whose day it is, and to beg through their merits the grace to attain to the perfection you require of me.

I offer it in thanksgiving to you for my Vocation to Religion, and for all the helps you have therein provided me for my Salvation and Sanctification, and beg the grace to love you perfectly in this life, and eternally in the other, and a happy death.

Lastly, I offer it for the intentions you would have me offer it up for, and for all those I ought to offer it for, to gain whatever pardon may be gained, and to beg the solace and deliverance of the poor souls in Purgatory, especially those that will be most for your glory.

Prayers

Prayers before Communion to the Blessed Trinity.

Eternal Father, I humbly beseech you, for the love that moved you to give us your Son, that you will prepare my heart to receive him worthily: enkindle in my soul as fervent desires to receive him, as you excited in the hearts of the Ancient Fathers, and other Holy Souls, who sighed most ardently for his coming.

My most dear Redeemer, I beg you, for that infinite Charity that moved you to come to save us, that you will prepare for yourself in my soul such a dwelling as shall be most pleasing to you. I should not have hoped for such a favour as to receive you, if you yourself did not ordain me to approach, give me then in giving me yourself all the dispositions required to receive you worthily; which I cannot have, unless you bestow them as a firm Faith, an ardent Love, and a profound Humility; let, dear Lord, this Feast be to me a pledge of that you keep for me in a blissful eternity.

Divine Spirit, I beg you to purify my heart, and enflame it with the fire of of your Love, to receive my dear Saviour worthily, who was conceived by your ineffable operation in the womb of the Blessed Virgin, that the Divine heart of Jesus may take delight in my Soul.

To our Blessed Lady.

Sacred Lady, worthy Mother of my Saviour, I beg you to obtain for me all those holy dispositions of heart, which I ought to have to receive worthily the Body and Blood of my Saviour, which he took from your Immaculate Substance: I beg it by the ardent wishes with which you expected the Coming of our Redeemer and Redemption of all mankind.

I beg it by the preparation you always brought to Divine Grace.

I beg it by the Humility, with the which you received the Word Incarnate in your Womb.

I beg it by the Love, with the which you embraced our dear Saviour, when come forth of your Sacred Womb.

I beg it by the Sorrow, with the which you received him into your arms taken down from the Cross.

I beg it by the Hope, with the which you laid him in the Sepulchre.

I beg it by the Preparation you brought to receive the Holy Ghost.

I beg it by the Devotion, with the which you received your dear Son in the most Blessed Sacrament.

I beg it by the Joy, with the which you was received by him into Heaven.

By all which I beg you will obtain me the grace to receive him worthily, and offer in place of what is wanting in me those dispositions, with the which you carried him nine months in your Womb, and by your intercession obtain that they may be applied to me.

Act of Faith.

My God, I have so firm a belief of your infinite Power and Goodness, that I doubt not of your having effectually inclosed your Body, Soul, and Divinity in this adorable Sacrament; your all-powerful Word has destroyed a Creature, and produced a God; grant it may destroy

ſtroy in me all that is mine and evil, and in place thereof produce what is yours, that your Spirit may live in me, and govern all my thoughts, words, and actions, that I may ſay with your Apoſtle, I live, not I, but Chriſt lives in me.

Act of Hope.

My God, ſince you ordain me to come, I will go with confidence to receive the honour you do me, and I hope you will fulfil your promiſe, that thoſe that eat this Bread ſhall live for ever, and that by means of this Divine Sacrament, you will grant me the grace of a pious Life and a happy Death, and accompliſh my deſire of loving you as I ought; and in giving me yourſelf, you will give me all the diſpoſitions to receive you worthily.

Act of Charity.

My Lord God, worthy of the love of all hearts, grant me the grace to love you with all mine; come into my heart and inflame it, that it may burn for ever in your love; you are wonderful in all your

your works, and much more in your love, to work such wonders for a creature so unworthy and undeserving as I am: come, dear Lord, and triumph over my heart; and let yours, when I shall receive you, inflame mine with your love, and convert it so wholly to you, that it may love nothing but you, or for you.

Act of Contrition.

My God, I am sorry and beg pardon for all my sins and offences, especially for my little respect in your Divine Presence, and my want of attention in all my Prayers, and for the little profit I have drawn from this Divine Sacrament, and my sloth and negligence in preparing for it.

Act of Humility.

O bread of Angels, in giving yourself to me, you become the food of beasts, for I am no better; for besides a sinner, I am a base self-lover. It is with confusion that I venture to receive the honour you not only invite me to, but command me to accept of; let then my obedience to it supply for my defects, for I acknowledge I am void of all virtue and good works, nor have I any fit dispositions in my soul to receive you with, and therefore must offer to you, in lieu of those dispositions that are wanting in me, those of your own Divine Heart, when you received yourself, which I beg you will accept of, and likewise those of your most Blessed Mother, when she received you, and of all your Saints and faithful Servants; and grant me those dispositions I ought to have, to render my soul grateful to you, which I cannot have unless you bestow them.

Act of Confidence.

My Lord, notwithstanding my Unworthiness, I will go with Confidence to receive you, because I am sick and infirm, and you assure me that the Physician is for them, and not for the well; and moreover, you being the Lamb of God that takes away the sins of the World, I will go in hopes that you will take away mine.

Act of Petition.

Dear Lord, before you instituted this Divine Sacrament, you begged of your Eternal Father, that admirable Effect which you desired it should produce, which is, that we might be one with you, as you and he is one ineffable Goodness. Grant, dear Lord, it may be so, that I may be united to you in sentiments, in inclinations, and in practice, imprint in the bottom of my soul the sentiments I ought to have of your Death and Passion, of which this Sacrament is a memorial. Grant me the grace that, for your sake, I may love what afflicts Nature, and will make it die, that I may live to you and for you.

Since your word is so powerful as to change bread into your Body, and wine into your Blood, shall not your Divine Person have the power to change me from what I am, into what you would have me be, and make me attain the end for which you created me, which is too sublime for me to acquire, unless strengthened by this Divine Food; it is therefore I go to receive it.

Act after Communion.

Most adorable Trinity, Father, Son, and Holy Ghost, I firmly believe I possess your Divinity; I adore you with all the extent of my heart, and most humbly thank you for visiting me, your poor unworthy creature; act so powerfully in me, as to change me from what I am, into what you would have me be.

Eternal Father, what shall I render you for this immense Treasure you have given me, in giving me your only Son? for in him I have all that can make me happy for time, and for all Eternity; it is he only that can worthily perform that duty, I therefore offer him to you in thanksgiving for it.

Receive him from me, and for me; for he is mine both by your gift and his, in acknowledgment of your supreme being and my dependence, and in thanksgiving for all your benefits bestowed on me, the poorest and meanest of your creatures, incapable of returning you due thanks for the least; receive his bitter Passion in satisfaction for all my sins, and pardon me them; however great my sins are, they cannot equal what he has suffered

fered for them; I beg his perfect obedience to your Will may satisfy for my neglecting or flothfully performing it.

I offer you all the merits of his Life, which are infinite, to obtain the grace to love you, as you require and command me; and the grace to persevere therein, as long as life, and the grace of a happy Death, which I can only hope from your pure Mercy and your Son's Merits, in whose Name I beg it; and he assures me, that whatever I ask in his Name, you will grant: I may not doubt of it since he has said it, nor will I: and since Faith can remove mountains, and confidence obtain what it hopes for, let this my Faith and Confidence in the Merits of your Son move your mercies to grant my petition, seeing also that the price I offer to obtain it, is infinite.

What thanks do I owe you, my Saviour, for giving me yourself and all your merits in this adorable Sacrament? which you do with an infinite desire of my salvation: I have nothing that I can render you in return but myself, which I here give with my whole heart, renewing the promises made both at my Baptism and my Profession.

Grant.

Grant, dear Saviour, that your Sacred Body and Blood, which I have received, may so fortify me, that I may by means thereof overcome all your enemies, and those of my Salvation, and remain faithful to your love during my whole life. I beg also the grace of a perfect consecration of myself to you, and the force and strength I have need of to support and undertake those sufferings and mortifications, which you would have me endure for my sins: grant me the grace that will nourish and make my soul to grow in all the perfection you require of me; and that grace purely gratuit of a final perseverance, which will bring me to the possession of you for all Eternity.

This, dear Lord, is the favourable time, the time of Salvation, since I possess you in my soul; and as nothing is impossible to you, for in one moment you can make in me that necessary and most desirable change, by changing my heart, and giving me a new one and a right spirit, which I beseech you to do, that I may love and praise you as I ought, and seek you with fervour, and accomplish with perfection your Divine Will, and direct all I do for your Glory.

Give

Give me the knowledge of what you require of me, and the grace to do it, govern all the motions of my heart, that it may always tend to you; grant that I may be meek and patient in adversities, and grateful to you in prosperity, and not dejected in affliction: never rejoice, but for what makes for your Glory; nor grieve, but for what makes to the contrary; desire but to please you, and fear nothing but to displease you: grant that I may love you above all things, give me the grace frequently to lift up my heart to you, who are my Sovereign Good; and when so unhappy as to offend you, immediately to grieve for it, so as to obtain your pardon; and since you require that I walk before you, and be perfect, give me a perfect obedience to all your ordinances, and a patience which never may complain or murmur, an humility rather interior than exterior, a confidence without presumption, a fear without despair: give to my soul a spiritual joy in all that relates to your service, a heart which entertains no unworthy affection, or evil intention; grant to my understanding to know you, and to my will

to

to love you, and fervour to serve you, and to desire nothing more than frequently to receive you in this Sacrament of love, and each time to come better prepared, and more worthy of that favour than other; grant that the remembrance of your sufferings may fasten me so to the cross with you, that being united to you here on earth, I may for ever enjoy you in Heaven.

My dear Saviour, since for my sake you have descended from Heaven into this adorable Sacrament to conduct me thither, permit me not to go astray from the perfection you require of me, but make me follow you, who are the way, the truth, and the life; I beg it by the love that obliged you to give your life for my Salvation, and that you will grant me the grace to know, love, and serve you, and to persevere in so doing till death.

I here render you the Right and Liberty you have given me over myself, and return for your goodness in visiting me your unworthy creature; dispose of me as you please, for I am yours, and desire to live but for you, and according to your will, and not mine; permit me not to follow the desires of my heart,
when

when contrary to yours, but make me walk the way of the perfection you require of me.

Most adorable Trinity, Father, Son, and Holy Ghost, in view of my obligations to you, and in gratitude for them, I here in your Presence renew the Promises made for me at Baptism, and those I made at my profession, which I beg pardon for unfaithfully observing, and the grace that I may faithfully observe them for the future.

Pardon, dear Lord, my sins and offences, and the faults I have committed, in unworthily receiving you, for want of a due preparation: I beg it in your name, and therefore hope you will grant it, for it would be a new offence for me to doubt of your mercy, which I beg I never may be guilty of.

I recommend to you all those that have desired my Prayers, or that I am on any account obliged to pray for, grant them all those graces that are necessary for them, and accomplish in them all your merciful providence has designed them.

Most Sacred Lady, worthy Mother of my dear Saviour, it is my duty to return you

you thanks for giving me your Son in this adorable Sacrament, which I most humbly do, and beg you will thank him for me, and obtain me the grace always worthily to receive him. You are the Mother of my Salvation, and Treasurer of all the graces of your Son, and his Holy Mother; it is by your means that he grants them to some, and more abundantly to others: obtain for me all those you know I stand in need of: I consecrate my heart to you, it is to your Son's and your Glory, that I dedicate all I am capable of; obtain that my heart may be so fixed in your Son's and your love, that it may not be in the power even of Hell to withdraw me from your love and service, or make me do any thing unworthy of the honour I have now received. *Amen.*

The remaining time you may employ the three powers of your soul; your memory, in calling to mind all the benefits you have received of his merciful goodness, and thanking him for them; your understanding, in reflecting on the greatness of them, especially this you have now received; and your will in acts of love to him.

You may also expose to him the evils you groan under, and how they threaten death to your soul, and the corruption of your heart, your self-love, and want of courage; that seeing the grievances of your wounds, he may be moved to cure them.

Aspirations which may serve during the Day.

When, my God, shall I be all yours, by an entire fidelity to your will?

Take from me all that may be opposite to your Glory: Let the fire of your love consume all that is amiss in me.

How comes it, dear Lord, that having so often fed on you, I am yet so weak as to be overcome by the least difficulty?

A Preparation for Communion, by commemorating the Death and Burial of Christ.

None can doubt but that, of all other Preparations for Communion, that of the Death and Burial of our Lord is the best, as being the most suitable to our Lord's design, since he bids us do it in the memory of his Death: Both his Death and his

his Burial is represented in Holy Mass; the latter by the Communion of the Priest and the Communicants.

The Altar is Calvary, where Christ offers the same Sacrifice as on the Cross, and our hearts are the Sepulchres which he has chosen to be laid in, and will sanctify, if we receive him with the dispositions we ought.

This Preparation contains two parts; the one is to purify our souls from sin, the other is to adorn it with Acts of virtue. As to the first, it may begin from the time we have been to confession: It consists in purifying our souls from sin, whereby we have rendered it an unfit sepulchre for our Lord to be laid in, and by a great care not to commit the least sin, nor to defile it any more.

From time to time we may say, dear Lord, your Sepulchre was neat and clean, but my heart is far otherways; for tho' it has been washed in Confession with your precious Blood, yet the root of ill habits remains still in me; for your own sake, I beg you will purify it from all that displeases you

The second duty is to adorn our hearts with virtues, which is done by embracing all

all occasions, which shall offer of practising them, and by performing all our spiritual duties with more fervour, and by frequent aspirations; begging our Lord to bestow whatever may render our hearts a more fit habitation for him to repose in.

Our Intentions for Communion. The same as before.

To the Blessed Trinity before Communion.

Eternal Father, I beg you, for the love which moved you to give your Son, that you will bestow on me all the graces I stand in need of worthily to receive him.

Divine Saviour, who, out of your infinite Charity, have not only given your Life for me, but yourself to me in this adorable Sacrament, give me all the dispositions I ought to have worthily to receive you. I offer you the dispositions with the which you received yourself, when you instituted this adorable Sacrament, and those with the which your Blessed Mother and your faithful Servants received

received you with: Accept of them in lieu of those that are wanting in me.

Divine Spirit, by whose operation my Lord was conceived in the Womb of his Blessed Mother, create in me those dispositions which will render my soul a fit habitation for him.

To our Blessed Lady.

Most Sacred Lady, Mother of my Saviour, and my dear Mother, take pity of my poverty and want of all good, and for the sake of your dear Son, send me of yours what is wanting in me to receive worthily your dear Son. It concerns you, that he be received as he ought to be: You know that I have nothing of my own, whereby I can do so. Shew yourself a Mother to me in this occasion, by supplying for what is wanting in me, it is what I most humbly beg of you.

Act of Faith.

I believe, my God, what Faith teaches me, that your infinite Goodness has made you descend from Heaven to come to me, under the accidents of Bread; left the brightness

brightness of your Glory should hinder me from approaching you, come to take possession of my heart as of your Kingdom; and to animate me with your spirit, that I may live of your life: It is for that I desire, above all things, to receive you, accomplish it in me, according to your designs.

After Contrition.

I am heartily sorry, and beg pardon for my sins, especially for my little respect, and for wandering in my thoughts when in your real presence, and for my continual infidelities to your graces; for all which I beg pardon, by the merits of the Blood you shed for them.

Act of Love.

No thought, dear Lord, can be more sweet than to think of your Love expressed in all you have suffered for me, since it gives me grounds to hope that you will pardon my sins, having satisfied to the Justice of your Eternal Father for them; you have had the goodness to make a transport of all your merits, which are infinite to him for me: The price you have given is of more worth and value, than all the goods of grace and glory I can hope for, or he bestow. How great is my obligation to love you, which I desire to do with my whole heart, and to seek in all things to please you, and to refuse nothing, however painful and hard, that you require of me.

Act of Humility.

Though my unworthiness, my God, terrifies me, your Goodness re-assures when I hear you say, Come to me, all you that are burdened with the weight of your miseries, and I will ease you; which invitation makes me forget, dear Lord, what I am, and go with Confidence, and with an assurance of pleasing you by so doing, as also, because, bid by those that holds your place to approach, notwithstanding my unworthiness, I therefore do and hope by it to obtain that necessary grace to overcome what hinders my advancement in the way of perfection.

Dear Lord, say to my soul when you enter it, this day Salvation is made to it, by granting me grace to love you only, and to desire and seek your Glory in all I do, do, and to dwell with you on Mount Calvary, by a constant remembrance of your sufferings and gratitude for the same; and when you have given yourself to me, take my soul with yourself in it.

Act after Communion.

I firmly believe I have received, and now possess the Body of my Lord, that was all covered with wounds for my salvation, and being dead for me, was laid in a sepulchre. I adore, my Lord, all those Sacred Wounds, and thank you for the profusion of the Blood you shed from them for me, giving me even to the last drop.

What can I think or say, dear Lord, at the most afflicting sight, since you received all those Wounds for me? and what renders it more afflicting is, that you received them in the house of my heart.

Give me, dear Lord, tears, both to bewail your sufferings and my sins, the unhappy cause of them; and since you suffered them all for me, apply the merits of them to my soul, that it may produce fruits worthy of them.

Grant

Grant that I may enjoy the effects of all you have merited me by your Passion; give me your Spirit, your Grace, and your Love, that I may love you alone, that have loved me to such a degree as to give your Blood and Life for me: fortify my weakness, and strengthen my will in good, that I may so operate with fidelity in the manner you require of me, as that I may be a victim of your Will.

Nothing has been capable, dear Lord, to hinder you from being all mine, neither Heaven, nor your Divinity, nor the gibbet of the Cross: grant me the grace, that nothing may hinder me from being all yours, to whom I owe myself both for Creation and Redemption.

It was never heard that in your mortal life you lodged with any, which you did not liberally reward with your gifts; I beg you will do the same to your present Habitation, which is my heart: let the touch of yours, which consecrates all things, sanctify my heart that it may be grateful to you.

Anima Christi Sanctifica me.
Corpus Christi salva me.
Sanguis

Sanguis Christi inebria me.
Aqua Lateris Christi lava me.
Passio Christi conforta me.
O Bone Jesu exaudi me.
Intra tua Vulnera absconde me.
Ne permittas me separari a te.
Ab Hoste maligno defende me.
In hora mortis meæ voca me.
Et jube me venire ad te.
Ut cum Sanctis tuis laudem te.
In secula seculorum. Amen.

I am poor, miserable, and weak, and of myself can do nothing; but with your grace, nothing is impossible to me: my life is all human, I know not if I even am, but this I know, that I am most miserable to live after such a manner: change, dear Lord, my life, and live in me, and let me live but for you, you can do it, that can do all things, and I hope and beg you will.

You see the danger I am in; hold me with your all-powerful hand that I fall not: direct me with your Spirit that I stray not; defend me, dear Lord, from myself, and permit me not to follow my irregular inclination and my own will, since it separates me from you;

you; make me sensible what ought to be the life of one that feeds on you, and give me the grace that mine may be such.

I beg that your Divine Presence may so fortify me in your love, that I may overcome all the enemies of it, and make daily more and more progress in it, and that having given yourself to me, you will give me the grace to give myself entirely to you, and that nothing may ever separate me from you.

I consecrate to you my soul and body, that you may sanctify both my actions and sufferings, that you may render them meritorious; my desires and good resolutions, that you may sustain them by your grace; my designs and undertakings, that you may bless them; my life and my death, that you may sanctify them; and above all, I offer you my heart, that you may enflame it, and reign for ever in it.

Take, dear Lord, my heart, and leave me your spirit, for how can I live when I see you dead, unless you leave me your spirit? that it may live in me, and make me to live for you only, and deplore the remainder of my days, in the

bitterness

bitterness of my heart, your death and my sins, which have been the cause of it, for which I most humbly beg pardon.

I beg, dear Lord, that you will grant me the victory over my passion, especially that which most opposes my Sanctification, and makes me unfaithful to your Love; remove all obstacles to your designs, and permit me not to be so ungrateful, after what you have done for me, as to refuse to live for you, whatever it must cost me.

Your Apostle tells me, that I am not my own but yours, you having bought me at a great price, which is more certain than certainty itself, and more true than all truths. Nothing can please me more than this assurance, that I am all yours and not my own, my soul does infinitely rejoice thereat. I am yours by an infinity of titles, you having redeemed me and delivered me, and spared my life, when I was guilty of death, from which time you tell me that I ceased being my own and become yours; may I ever be so; it is in that consists my comfort and my happiness.

Though by necessity I am yours, I will be so by my free choice, and therefore I
bequeath

bequeath my Soul to you, my moſt dear Redeemer—my body to your ſweet Providence—my heart to your Love—my liberty to your Will—my whole being to your Glory——all my good and bad thoughts, words, and deeds to your Mercies—my Life and my Death to your Providence—all my affairs, both Spiritual and Temporal, to the Protection of your moſt dear Mother.

My Lord and my God, ſince you are pleaſed to be all mine, I beg you will give me the grace to be all yours: Whoſe ſhould I be but yours, my Creator and Redeemer? who has ſo many rights over me, and to whom I totally owe myſelf. I bid adieu, therefore, to all Creatures, to dedicate myſelf wholly to the good Will and Pleaſure of you, my God and Creator.

Moſt Sacred Lady, Mother of my Saviour, and my moſt dear Mother, you was preſent at the Sepulchre of your Son, and with your Hand and Advice aſſiſted them to bury him. I beg your aſſiſtance for that effect, that I may bury him in my heart, which by Holy Communion is become a myſtical Sepulchre of his.

Help

Help me to render him all the duties I owe him, in imitation of your example; with what tender affection did you receive him into your Arms, when taken down from the Cross? With what grief did you behold all his Wounds? you washed them with your tears, which flowed in great abundance from your eyes; you kissed them with profound respect, and with the bosom of your Love you imbalmed them; obtain me the grace to do the same, and not only to weep for Compassion of his Sufferings, but also for my sins, the unhappy cause thereof: and as my poverty affords me not the sweet perfumes of virtues to imbalm him with, I beg you, as my most dear Mother, that you will offer him yours to supply for what is wanting in me.

When you saw him laid in the Sepulchre, how greatly did your grief increase, to see yourself deprived of his Sacred Body? you would willingly have remained by him at the Sepulchre; but because it was God's Will you should not, you separated yourself from him, teaching me, by your Example, to deprive myself of whatever is most dear to me, when God requires it.

My

My dear Saviour, I offer you the sweet perfumes of all virtues, with the which your Blessed Mother imbalmed you, and I wish it were in my power, tho' it cost me never so much, to anoint your Sacred Body with the same.

I beg, by the merits of your Sacred Mother, to grant me the grace to love you and her, so as that nothing may be able to withdraw me from it.

Mother of my Saviour, accept of me for your Child, and bury me in the Wounds of your dear Son, and obtain for me, that I may live in a faithful observance of all the duties of a Spouse of his.

Your rest, dear Lady, was in Labours; your delight was in the Cross, and your Life was in the Death of Jesus; obtain for me by the merits of your Son, that I may imitate you.

SEC. IX.

Reflections for our first awaking, when we design to receive our Lord as Father.

Considering him as your Father, and yourself as his most ungrateful child, and

and desirous of returning to your duty, say, *I will arise and go to my Father*, do it with speed, and with a great confidence that he will receive and forgive you.

While you are dressing, keep your thoughts more or less upon the same subject.

Before Communion.

Reflect that *that* Lord, whom Heaven and earth reverences as their God, has adopted you for his child, and requires that you should esteem and love him as your Father. Hence take courage to go to him, for such is his love, that he is not content to call himself and to be our Father, but because a Mother's love is more tender, he compares himself to a Mother, saying, that though peradventure she may forget the infant she brought forth, yet will he not be unmindful of us, for he has us written in his hand; and then again, as a Mother makes much of the child she nourishes at her breast, so will he cherish and comfort us. What motives for confidence! let us then believe that since he is our Father,

Father, he cannot but act like a Father, if we behave ourselves like good children, asking him pardon, and being truly sorry for having offended him, which if we do, he will entirely forgive us, and receive us to his embraces with tenderness, like to the Father of the prodigal Son. With this assurance let us rise and go to Communion, saying to ourselves, *I will arise and go to my Father.*

After Communion.

Consider that your most merciful Father has received you into favour, and in token of it has made this great banquet for you, a greater cannot be made! for which return him the best thanks you are able, and with great humility say,

O my Lord and merciful Father, it had been sufficient, if you had only permitted me to have dwelt in some corner of your House among your meanest servants, which had been more than I deserved; but you in place of that have acted like what you are, a God of infinite Mercy!

How great is your goodness to take upon you the Name and Office of a Father,

Father, in regard of duft and afhes, which I am! how can I poffibly give a condign welcome to fuch a Father, or exprefs the joys my Heart is full of, to receive you into it! make me a Child worthy of fo good a Father, and imprint the character of it in my Heart and actions. Pardon all I have offended you in, and give me the Spirit of Adoption which may make me love you, and have recourfe to you as to my Father; grant me alfo your fear, which may keep me from ever difpleafing you in the leaft.

SEC. X.

Reflections for our Firft Awaking, when we confider him as our Paftor.

Conceive a great joy that Chrift your good Paftor will come this day to vifit you in Holy Communion; and be affured that he will fulfil all the duties of a good Paftor in your regard.

While you drefs, entertain your thoughts upon that fubject.

Before Communion.

Reflect that Christ your good Pastor is descended from Heaven, and in this Sacrament, to seek and save you, who have most ungratefully strayed from him; and that not once only, or a hundred times, but as often as you have sinned. Acknowledge that of yourself you are incapable either to find your Pastor, or the way to him, did not he in his mercy come to you, which in this Sacrament he is pleased to do, and will perform all the duties of the best of Pastors, as he declares by the Mouth of his Prophet, promising, *That he himself will seek and visit his sheep, &c. and in the most plentiful Pastures will he feed them, &c. that which was gone astray he will bring back, that which was broken he will bind up, that which was weak he will strengthen,* and that which was fat and strong he will keep: ponder every particular, for each is full of pith; and encouraged by the same, go with confidence to receive your dear Pastor.

After

After Communion.

Adore and thank your Divine Paftor for coming to feek you who fo little deferve this his tender concern for you. Admire his Love! he ftands in no need of you, yet feeks you as if his happinefs depended upon you! Acknowledge his goodnefs in feeding you with his own moft precious Body and Blood, which he does with fo great a Love, that he even threatens Death to thofe that will not approach to receive him.

Say to him, your mercies, Lord, exceed all thought. I can never thank and praife you fufficiently for your great goodnefs, in making yourfelf my Food, and feeking me when gone aftray, which I have fo often done! and alfo for placing me in your richeft paftures; nay, in your fheepfold Holy Religion, in which you place your Elect Flock, and from whence (if I hinder you not) you will carry me to your fheepfold of Eternal Blifs; for all which I owe you more gratitude than all Hearts are capable of.

Pardon my ungrateful withdrawing myfelf from your Conduct, and making ufe even of your Benefits to offend you.

Though

Though there is nothing in me, dear Lord, that can merit your mercy, yet knowing you are so bountifully good, and so inclined to forgive, I here with prostrate Heart implore your Pardon for all my past Ingratitudes, and beg moreover this unlimited favour, that you will imprint anew your mark upon me, to make appear that I am of those sheep which your mercies will place on your Right Hand at Judgment. Let your Cross distinguish me, not a necessary bearing it, (which all must do) but a voluntary embracing it for Love of you: Grant that I may constantly hear and obey your voice whenever it calls me.

SEC. XI.

Reflection for our First Awaking when we receive him as our Physician.

Reflect that Christ, your Divine Physician, will come this day to visit you, to whose power and skill no disease is incurable. Rise with great Confidence of obtaining your Soul's Health, since he requires no more to cure us, but an acknowledgment

knowledgment of your infirmity, and a real desire to be cured.

Before Communion.

Consider that when Christ was in the World, none ever came to him to be cured who did not obtain it. No sooner had the Centurion told him of his sick Servant, but presently he answered that he would come and cure him. And to the Lepers, who only said, *Lord, if you will you can make us clean*; he answered, *I will that you be clean*; and to several others he offered Health, without being asked.

By all which move yourself to a great Confidence of obtaining the cure of your soul's diseases: It is chiefly for that end he desires to come to us, as his own Words express, saying, the healthy have no need of a Physician, but those that are infirm; signifying thereby that his chief office is to be a Physician of souls; and to the end we may be healed of all our infirmities, he has made a Medicine of his own Flesh and Blood, and has left it us in this Sacrament, that by receiving it we may be cured of all our diseases.

O

O what a Physician! and what a remedy! who can doubt of being cured, for he not only cures past sins, but preserves us from future ones: Let us then with confidence rise and go to receive him, since he declares that he comes for the sick and infirm, as such let us approach him that he may cure us.

After Communion.

Conformable to the foregoing consideration, entertain your Divine Physician. Confide that only the touch of his Sacred Body will effect the perfect cure of all your soul's disease. Return him infinite thanks for taking this office upon him, and for his charity in visiting so poor and loathsome a sick soul as yours is, and beg him to excuse the stench which your diseases send forth, and which would strike horror to a less goodness than his.

Lay open your maladies to him as well as you can; and if your ignorance is so great that you know them not, or cannot declare them, beg him that knows them to cure them, and to cure the blindness of your understanding; to molify the hardness of your heart as to good; to stop the
impetuous

impetuous course of your will to evil; to purge you of those hateful dispositions of pride and envy; and to root up self-love, the source of all evils.

SEC. XII.

Reflections for our First Awaking, when we consider him as our soul's Guest.

Reflect on those words our Lord spoke to Zaccheus, and suppose the same are said to you: *Come down in haste, for this day I will abide in your house.* Conceive a great desire of that happiness, and rise with speed.

Before Communion.

Consider that the same Lord whom you are to receive, complained to his Disciples that the foxes had holes and the birds their nests, but the Son of man had no where to repose his head, having been refused entertainment, when in the shape of man: he has cloathed himself with the form of bread, that so he may enter your heart, and make your soul his mansion.

Acknowledge

Acknowledge the poorness and vileness of the lodging of your heart to receive and lodge so great a God. Say to him, Tho' you are pleased to say, dear Lord, that your delights are to be with the children of men, yet how is it possible you can take delight in so poor a habitation as mine is? therefore, for your own sake, give me what may render my heart an agreeable dwelling to you, for unless you bestow it, I cannot have it.

The desire you express of being my guest, encourages me to receive you, tho' I am most unworthy: you expect not an invitation from me, but invite yourself, and ever press to come, assuring me that you are ever calling at the door of my heart, and that if I will open to you, you will come in and sup with me, and let me sup with you.

After Communion.

Welcome that Lord to this poor home of mine; welcome my soul's felicity, thrice happy hour which has blessed me with the presence of my God! a greater Happiness I cannot receive on earth, nor you give, because you give yourself. I
bless

bless your mercies, and again bid you as welcome as a heart, filled with love and gratitude, can do!

But when I reflect on myself, how can I welcome you! my soul is defiled with sin, and my house is nothing but a den of beasts, and hideous monsters! though for yourself you are highly welcome; yet in regard to what I am, I must desire you, with St. Peter, to depart from me to those holy souls who are prepared to receive so great a guest. Leave this den of mine, for it is better I should perish in misery, than entertain your sanctity in so prophane a heart.

But if your goodness is such that notwithstanding you are willing to stay, chase from me all you dislike in me, and all that is hurtful to me; purify my heart, or create a new one in me. Dear Lord, you know my poverty, and therefore you cannot expect that I can offer you any thing but requests, your coming therefore cannot be to take, but to give me entertainment. Your entering my heart is not so much to be my guest as to make me yours. Say to my soul what you did to Zaccheus, *this day salvation is made on this house:* you can as easily

easily bestow salvation on me, as on him, and it is chiefly for that end you come; speak then that word of comfort to my soul, and it shall be for ever blessed, and pardon the bad entertainments I have given you, whenever I have had the honour to receive you: and also all the faults I have ever committed; and besides your pardon for the past, give me amendment for the future, and such holy thoughts and amorous desires, as are fitting to entertain so great a goodness, and so good a God.

SEC. XIII.

Reflections at our First Awaking, when we receive him as our VIATICUM.

Imagine this to be the day in which you are to take your great journey from time to eternity. Reflect, with gratitude and confidence, that Christ himself will be your Viaticum, say to your soul,

Arise, let us go and die with Jesus.

Before Communion.

Consider that in this Sacrament is truly contained the Bread of Life, it being the Body of Christ, who is life itself, and gives life to the dead: he comes to you, to enable you to go to him; and to make your journey from earth to heaven, from time to a happy Eternity. O infinite Goodness! I can fear no evil if you are with me; I will approach you with confidence, confiding, that since you give yourself to me here, you will not refuse yourself to me in heaven: and I hope your coming is to lead me to that happiness, and render me worthy of it, by applying to my soul the merits of the Blood you shed, which I am going to receive.

Come then, dear Lord, but before you enter my Heart, forgive me all my offences. I wish I could by my present devotion and fervour supply for all my defects of former Communions; if you bestow it on me I shall; it is what I humbly beg. Grant, or receive (in lieu of what is wanting in me) those Sacred Dispositions with which you received yourself, and those with which your

Blessed Mother, and all your servants, have received you.

After Communion.

Adore Christ in your breast, with sentiments of a respectful fear, considering him as your Judge; and then reflecting that he is not less your Saviour, assuming a fresh confidence, say to him,

Is it not in you that you would have me place my whole confidence? I do, dear Lord, for I know your Divine Heart is mine, and for me; this assures me against all fears, and makes me hope that your Judgment will be, in my regard, a Judgment of love and mercy.

Blessed be the Father of Mercies for giving me my Redeemer for Judge, without which, what could I have hoped for! O turn your eyes from the evils I have done, and only look on what your Goodness has done for me. I acknowledge there is nothing in me which is not criminal, but there is not one of my sins for which you have not shed your Blood to wash away its stain. Permit me not to be lost, after having cost you so dear! my soul is in your hands, which is all my confolation; it is infinitely more fecure than in my own! by the Precious Blood you fhed for it, grant it may never be feparated from you.

I offer my life, and all I fhall leave by dying, as a Sacrifice to you. Permit not death to feize on me fo fuddenly as to find me unprovided. Sanctify my death, and grant I may die humble, penitent, and perfectly fubmiffive to your Will; heartily pardoning all, and receiving pardon of all my offences; fortified by your Grace, and Holy Sacraments, with due fentiments of gratitude. Such a death I ardently defire, grant it me as foon as you pleafe; and to obtain it, and a favourable fentence, I beg your grace that for the remainder of my life I may obferve all you ordain me for that effect, which is, *If I judge not, I shall not be judged; if I pardon all, I shall receive pardon of all my fins;* this, dear Lord, I do with my whole heart.

O my Judge, but more Father than Judge! if it depends but on my obferving thefe articles to fecure me your favour, and to remain for ever in it, behold me with your grace, ready to perform them; one favour I beg, which is that

that you will tarry with me, my dear Saviour, becauſe my days are almoſt ſpent, and this viſible ſun will ſoon ſet to me: O! bring me to the place where you yourſelf are the Eternal Lamp.

Leave me not till I breathe forth my Soul, which I now recommend into your Sacred Hands, that it may remain for ever with you. Amen.

Anſwers to the Objections againſt frequent Communions. Out of St. Francis of Sales.

If worldlings aſk you (ſays the Saint) why you communicate ſo often? tell them you do it to learn to love God; to be purified from your imperfections, to be comforted in your afflictions, and to find reſt, repoſe, and eaſe in your weakneſſes. Tell them that two ſorts of perſons ſhould communicate very often; the *Perfect*, becauſe being well diſpoſed, they would wrong themſelves did they not approach to the very ſource of Perfection; and the *Imperfect*, that they may aſpire to Perfection; the Strong, leſt they become weak; and the Weak, to become ſtrong; the Sick to be cured, and the Healthy to be preſerved from ſickneſs.

nefs. Tell them that for your own part, as one very imperfect, weak, and sick, you have great need to communicate often with him, who is your only Perfection, Strength, and Health. Tell them that those who have not many worldly affairs should communicate often, because they have good leisure; and those who have many temporal occupations should likewise do so, because they stand in need of it; and that he that labours much, must eat often, and strengthen himself with hearty food. Tell them that you receive the Blessed Sacrament to learn to receive it well; for no man can do an action well which he has not often practised; therefore communicate as often as you can with Counsel and Advice of your Ghostly Father.

INDEX.

INDEX.

	Page
OF the great Advantages and Benefits of Prayer	3
The Necessity of Prayer, chiefly mental	6
Of Preparation for Prayer	13
What we are to observe in Time of Prayer	15
For after Prayer	16
Preludes which may serve for any Meditation	18
A Compendium of mental Prayer	19
Different Manners of Meditating	20
How to perform an Act of Thanksgiving well	28
The Manner of making Colloquies	29
Some Methods which may serve in Desolation and Dryness	35
Motives to raise in us a high esteem of the Divine Office	38
Of the remote Preparation for the Divine Office	42
The immediate Preparation for the Divine Office	46
Several Manners of keeping our thoughts attentive to God during the Divine Office	48
Motives to incline us to frequent Visits of the most Blessed Sacrament	55
Of visiting the most Blessed Sacrament	59
Manners of visiting the Blessed Sacrament for every Day of the Week	60
How advantageous it is to keep ourselves in the Presence of God	84

INDEX.

	Page
A Practice of the Presence of God, by Means of Faith, Hope, Charity, &c.	89
Of Faith	91
Of Hope	98
Of Charity	102
Of Conformity to the Will of God	104
An Oblation or Profession of an entire Submission to God's Will	109
Motives for loving and honouring our Blessed Lady, and to raise a high Esteem for the Devotion of the Beads	111
A Method on the Words of the Angelical Salutation	115
A shorter Method on the same	120
Another Manner of reciting the Beads	121
A Method for saying the Rosary	123
A Practice of Devotion to our Angel Guardian	132
Of Spiritual Confession	136
Of Sacramental Confession	139
Three Days Preparation for Communion before all great Feasts	154
Three Days Preparation for Communion before the Feasts of our Blessed Lady	159
On ordinary communicating Eves	162
For Communion	165
General Intentions for Communion	167
For the Mass before Communion	171
The Necessity and Advantages of employing well the Time after Communion	179
How we ought to employ those precious Moments	180

A

INDEX.

	Page
A Manner of performing the same	181
Another Manner of Entertainment after Communion	191
Intentions for Communion	197
A Manner of receiving our Lord under the Notion of Father	228
A Manner of receiving him as Pastor	231
A Manner of receiving him as our Physician	234
A Manner of receiving him as our Soul's Guest	237
A Manner of receiving him as our Viaticum	240

A PRAYER

A PRAYER

FOR OUR KING AND COUNTRY.

MOST adorable Lord Jesus Christ, Saviour of the World, *God of Hosts, and Prince of Peace,* look down with eyes of compassion upon our manifold miseries: we confess our heinous transgressions; we turn to you with contrite hearts; to you, O God! our *Refuge* and *Defence: Remember not, O Lord! our or our Parents Offences, nor take vengeance of our sins:* regard us, as you are our Pastor, as the sheep of your flock, and as the poor remains of your ancient sheepfold in England: *Be mindful of your congregation, which you have possessed from the beginning:* O Jesus, be to us a Jesus; be to us a *Saviour;* hear, O God, our Prayer; let our cry come unto you: we believe in you; we call upon your Holy Name; let us not be confounded; spare us, O Lord! spare your People, lest your enemies may say, *Where is their God? your Altars are polluted; your inheritance destroyed; but you, O my Lord, how long?*

Inspire,

PRAYER.

Inspire, O JESUS, with your Holy Grace; endue with your Holy Spirit the Missioners of our nation consecrated to your service; renew in them the wisdom, zeal, and piety of their Predecessors; purify their lives, second their words, and sanctify their mystery, that in and by you the good may be confirmed; the wandering may be reclaimed; and the spotless Religion formerly planted, may once more revive and blossom in our Land.

Shower down your blessings, O bountiful God, upon your anointed *our* SOVEREIGN *King George,* and *all the Royal Family.* And as you have mercifully pleased to call them to the unity of your Faith and bosom of your Church; let them see that you are *their Safeguard;* grant them Constancy, grant them Fidelity to your Divine Graces, and grant them perseverance in your Love and Service: direct them in their Councils; strengthen them in their Enterprizes; and render them victorious over all their Enemies; re-establish them in their Kingdoms, and give them many years to enjoy the same. This we beg by the Passion and Merits of JESUS CHRIST your only Son, who lives and reigns with you in union of the Holy Ghost for ever and ever. *Amen.*

www.ingramcontent.com/pod-product-compliance
Lightning Source LLC
Chambersburg PA
CBHW031730230426
43669CB00007B/312